PAINTING
THE
WHOLE
PICTURE

Portrait of an Artist with Epilepsy

ALSO BY JOSHUA HOLMES

The Grand Mal Series

grand mal
seizure
status
trigger

The Design Series

design to kill
design for justice
design to escape
design for honor
design for power

Stand Alone Works

memory lapse
shattered lung

PAINTING
THE
WHOLE
PICTURE

Portrait of an Artist with Epilepsy

JOSHUA HOLMES

JⱣⱧ

JAHbookdesign | York

* I have tried to recreate events, locales and conversations from my memories of them. In order to maintain
their anonymity in some instances I have changed the
names of individuals and places, I may have changed
some identifying characteristics and details such as physical properties, occupations and places of residence.

* Some names and identifying details have been changed
to protect the privacy of individuals.

For my Parents and Grandparents

AUTHOR'S NOTE

MOST OF MY friends and family know me as the quiet, solemn guy in the corner who watches things from afar and only talks when I know I can contribute or speak confidently about a given topic. My closer friends know I wear my emotions on my sleeve, that I have a dry sense of humor, comfortably share corny jokes, and I'm fiercely loyal.

That said, I value my privacy and yet I'm a hard-working, passionate creative. I love to share my gifts. I love when others are blessed by my work, my thoughts, my art, and my writing. I primarily wrote fiction, to express myself in third person. But the Lord convicted me to do a nonfiction piece, to confidently tell my story, not only to share the realities of epilepsy, cerebral palsy, and partial blindness, but also to emphasize the truth that conditions don't have to be hindrances, that in Christ one can accomplish all kinds of things. And, more than that, a person doesn't have to achieve things conventionally. If He wills it, I've learned, your life will unfold in ways that far exceed your expectations.

And so, through this compilation of life events, this novel, I hope to encourage everyone, including my friends with epilepsy and other conditions. We all go through difficulties, but with faith, with the right perspective, and with commitment, we all can thrive.

Enjoy my story. It's one of a kind.

Joshua

PAINTING
THE
WHOLE
PICTURE
Portrait of an Artist with Epilepsy

PROLOGUE
IT'S TIME

I WAS AGAIN in my bedroom, at my drawing desk before a rickety easel displaying a blank, suede canvas, not only mulling over the start of a fresh pastel piece, but also over the new certainties that rang out in the silence like shifting church bells.

I'd come to many realizations while drawing over the years, religious or otherwise, for the pastime was my release. I could make something out of nothing, develop my interpretations to my heart's content, introduce more beauty into the world, and still listen for God and allow my mind to wander and process.

I'd even realized, more recently, that some things evaded me simply because I over-thought. Because I reasoned until I was blue in the face. That if I just took a deep breath, slowed, and prayed, I would more quickly hear and understand.

I tried to put in around ninety hours per piece. That time frame yielded the quality of work I felt comfortable sharing. I started by angling my floor lamps just so for adequate lighting, positioning my chair, and then sketching in the subject's anatomy.

I subsequently built upon the sketch, cleaning out excess lines, accentuating the necessary ones. Rounding off rough circles and hard edges. And then selecting my color palette.

To achieve depth, I stacked layers on the suede like clothes in a drawer. As if on cue, I heard those crystal clear church bells ring louder. Intrigued, I swiveled left and right, looked at the light coming through the window, feeling affirmed.

Again facing my canvas, I darkened my darks, and lightened my lights. Identified and softened the middle tones. I enhanced my portrait with more confidence, and it seemed I continued to receive affirmation for taking the right steps.

Forty-five hours in, the certainties chimed so starkly, I stopped working there in my quiet bedroom and intently listened. I stood and paced. The direction I always longed for seemed so apparent and logical. I felt a peace about it. I knew God had spoken.

Above everything else, I heard Him say, "It's time to tell your story."

PART ONE

Birth Through High School
1980-1998

I
FIRST BORN

NINETEEN EIGHTY WAS a significant year. Ronald Reagan was elected. Pac-Man was introduced. Mount St. Helens erupted. Jon Lennon was shot. And my parents, Robert and Julie Holmes, were celebrating their one-year anniversary, expecting my planned birth.

Together in Texas, at the Longview Hospital, they felt relief, the rough nine-month pregnancy fading away with my natural arrival.

"Congratulations," said Dr. Gore, the Southern, American-Asian physician. "You have yourself a healthy baby boy."

"Two and a half weeks early and still eight and a half pounds," said a veteran nurse.

"And his name?" said Dr. Gore.

Mom and dad spoke in unison. "Joshua Andrew Holmes."

I was born the first of three children. A hungry tike, I ate voraciously.

My appetite grew for four years at my nearby rental home, a modern duplex connected to our landlord's, Mr. Brown's, doughnut shop, a business my father ran.

Years later, when living in Pennsylvania, I'd officially receive a diagnosis of Cerebral Palsy (CP) and epilepsy. Later still, after more testing, I'd receive another diagnosis, called Poly Microscopic Gyra, which explained the rough pregnancy, suggesting I had a stroke the second month in utero.

As an infant, I solely crawled about on my left arm and leg, hand and foot. Due to atrophy, my right arm and leg, fingers and toes, were pulled tight, and I inevitably relied on the limbs and digits that worked.

Mom tested the use of my arm and fingers, pouring dry cereal in a bowl, having me reach and grasp for Cheerios with my weak side in my high chair. Cheerios continued to be a rehabilitative tool, forcing my body to do what didn't come innately.

Dad also 'patterned' my body. Upon learning of the technique from my grandma, he placed me on my back. Directing my limbs, he simulated the normal crawling movements for me. I imagine my grit was established then.

Mom later observed that I would randomly stare off. It was not usual, she recognized, informed the doctors who only suggested she look into it, and yet—without a formal diagnosis—I continued to stare. Even so, I developed like any other healthy toddler.

When older, I sometimes snuck into the shop early in the morning and grabbed my favorite treat, a blueberry cake doughnut. If blueberry cake wasn't available, I lifted a chocolate cake. Other days, I delivered a doughnut box to our friendly neighbors, the Edwards.

I was a happy child; Pictures of my sister, brother and me hugging, all in white-blonde hair and smiles, at different ages, seem to prove this. My memory isn't strong, but I have retained happy times.

I was born a creative, and a perfectionist, at that! Well, I wrote, read, and drew, it seems, from the beginning; As long as I can remember. And since I had a number of physical things that kept me from organized athletics, I thrived instead in the creative world.

Every day, mom required an hour of reading time. While my brother and sister weren't huge fans, often playing instead, I happily went to my room and read through book after book.

I don't know that I initially thought about writing, but it eventually crossed my mind. And in time I do recall drawing cartoons and jotting stories in a single-line, spiral notebook. I had a growing appetite for creativity.

A *York Daily Record* journalist on assignment took notice. One afternoon, at my proud parents' invite, she came to my house and interviewed mom and me. She went on to write a nice albeit melodramatic, small-town, biographical sketch about a uniquely determined boy, showcasing my early life obstacles, successes, and artwork. It was the first of two times I graced a newspaper.

In the accompanying photo, I lay on my stomach and intensely drew an animated duck. My reference was sewn onto one of mom's towels, which was spread out before me. The image spoke to my love for creativity, and my determination to rise above any challenge, no matter what.

2
FEVER

AT AGE TWO, the doctor stated my first ever shaking seizure was due to a fever. This was news, as it was different than the undiagnosed, random staring spells my mom previously noticed and mentioned.

"We should take him to the hospital," said my dad, standing before the stone fireplace, his concern reflecting in the flames. "To have him looked at."

"Yes," said my mother. "I agree." She rose from the contemporary blue couch.

Grandma took a deep breath. She had traveled by plane from Pennsylvania to our Texas home, to see her grandkids and help out.

Little did she know that, around midnight, while mom and dad cared for my brother Matt, a newborn, I would have a violent spell. My parents would awaken her from a deep sleep, to tell her and request more babysitting.

"I'll go start the car," said dad, jingling the keys on his index finger. "It's just down the road."

"We heard Josh from the living room and came as fast as we could."

Grandma then heard me gurgling in the background.

"Oh Julie," said grandma, reaching for my brother. "Now, now sweetheart. We will watch Matt here. Go on! This just breaks my heart!"

It broke her heart so much, I understand, that she later put her face to the floor in a separate room and wept. My Uncle Andy, who at age ten drove down by car with my grandpa, witnessed this and thought I had passed.

Mom transported me from the crib to the carrier, prepared me for travel, and left the house.

It was another arid, Texas night, the stillness thick, the moisture heavy. The armadillos congregated at the yard's edge, watching with glowing eyes as dad maneuvered around his parked motorcycle and pulled out of the driveway.

In the car, mom looked over at me, and placed the back of her hand to my forehead. "He's burning up, Bobby."

"Ok. Well, we're here."

Situated in the doctor's office, dad and mom anxiously waited. The square room was cramped and smelled of disinfectant.

The physician walked in soon after. He picked up a chart, looked at the information the nurses compiled. He then put on some latex gloves.

Completing an assessment of his own, he confirmed I was, in fact, sick, had a spiked temperature, and seized as a result.

"Febrile seizures are associated with young children," said the doctor, pulling the latex from his fingers, one digit at a time. "Early exposure to virus and vaccination can do it, an increased temperature manifesting, leading to the subsequent spell."

"This was worse than his other ones," said my mom.

"He shook and lost consciousness," said dad. "Made noise."

"They look disturbing, yes. But they are generally harmless," the doctor went on, tossing his plastic gloves.

"So Joshua will be alright, then?"

The doctor nodded and offered a brief smile.

"Of course," he said. "There are always extenuating circumstances. Some children even inherit a physical tendency to respond to fever in this way. Joshua, however, is not one of them."

My parents didn't pass down a predisposition. And after that night, I didn't have another febrile seizure. I did, however, share the virus.

A couple weeks later, my mom and grandma became gravely ill. Of the two, my grandma suffered a worse case that she struggled to kick.

Back in Huntingdon, my Aunt Laura questioned its origin, wondering about the severity, proposing that grandma simply missed Matt and me. But the dreaded fever proved otherwise.

In the years to come, until and after we moved from Longview, Texas to York, Pennsylvania, I would seize not because of a spiked temperature, but rather because of epilepsy, a congenital, pre-existing condition.

It would take another two years for a different doctor in Pennsylvania to accurately call my symptoms and conditions what they were.

3
MONKEY BARS

THE DAY I finally crossed the monkey bars was a milestone. I was around five or so. My parents and grandparents were there in the open back yard of our maroon, chicken farm rental, surrounding the swing set as I reached for the third to last rung. They cheered for me, and walked alongside me, as my body swayed back and forth like a loose branch in the wind.

It was a big deal, because until then my entire right side—still atrophied from CP—lacked the strength to hold on. It naturally wanted to withdraw. In the days leading up to it, I made several attempts where I successfully managed two or three bars, but then ran out of juice, lost my grip, and fell into the grass. I loathed falling, partially because it hurt but mostly because I hadn't accomplished what I set out to do. Oh, the frustration!

The task sometimes felt daunting and unattainable. Far away. To know what I wanted to do, and to watch what my body actually did were two different things. A battle, really.

And yet, time and again, I got up in that muggy, chicken stink, climbed the swing set, and tried to beat my obstacle. From the bars, you could see our landlord's olive and white-striped trailer to the left, the silver chicken factory straight back, and a horse stable to the right, sometimes Bear, the neighborhood St. Bernard, milling about, although my eyes were presently focused dead ahead in order to achieve the goal.

I know that God was there with my parents, grandparents and me, supporting and rooting for me too. I asked Jesus into my heart earlier that year following a puppet show at a Christian pre-school I attended instead of the recommended Easter Seals; Was proud of my decision to accept the Salvation invitation. I still remember how exciting that day was.

I was young, but I took it seriously, just as I took completing my monkey bar climb seriously. Just as I took everything I started seriously. I trembled as I closed in on the final two rungs. The metal ripped at my palm and fingers. For a split second, I managed to cling to the bar with my right arm, and then I quickly supported my weak side with my left. I shifted my weight to compensate.

I had to preserve my strength for the final bar. It was the hardest transition and demanded the most determination and physical strength. Mom and dad and grandma and grandpa cheered louder to push me to the end.

"Look at those muscles!"

"You're so close, buddy."

"So proud of you sweetie!"

I struggled yet imagined the celebration that would follow. The burn was severe, the fatigue nearly overwhelming. My insides quaked, but I at last latched onto the sixth bar. I hung there a moment, realizing what I'd just achieved, listening to the joy in the air, the cheers.

I then looked at my dad, who sported dark hair, a golden mustache, and an excited smile. I dropped into his arms and hugged him. I was exhausted. I made my rounds, hugging mom, grandma, and grandpa. I was also proud. The entire family was proud.

I had worked so hard. Pushed myself. And I saw my reward. Even so, it was just one of many challenges I'd face, and ultimately another on my list to conquer.

4
SHOELACES

I TIED MY first set of shoelaces the year of the *Discovery* space shuttle explosion. It jumps out at me, because—with the exception of *Little House on the Prairie*—I watched very little television as a child but did so that day. The event was a historical first, made national TV news, and ironically coincided with my accomplishment.

In the days leading up to lift off and the subsequent fireworks, while the NASA astronauts still lived, I spent a lot of time trying to make a knot. Well, I spent a lot of time trying to position my feet, trying to pull the strings taut, and then more time trying to hold still one loop, so I could securely wrap it.

There was a noticeable foot size differential. In width and length, my right foot was atrophied, an inch shorter and narrower. My right toes were smaller, weaker, and less agile, as well.

During my early attempts, I faced repeated instances where my left shoe was tied properly, the laces fastened, and where my right shoe was loose, more prone to come undone.

The difference in fit tested my perfectionist nature. Even then, my resolve was evident. I returned to the matter that discontented me, to attempt a more suitable outcome.

On separate occasions at different stores my parents, grandparents, and I looked for shoes that would save time, that were easier to prepare.

"We are looking for a pair with Velcro, Pap," said grammy.

"Yes Mom Mom," said gramps.

"And for the stretchy, coiled shoelace," said mom.

"It simplifies the process," said dad.

"I'll look too," I said.

We might get the laces," said mom. "But you remember our agreement, right?"

"I remember. You want me to learn how to lace everything first."

The thing was, I attended Mrs. Wert's kindergarten class; A bright carrot top with a love for Clifford the Big Red Dog and high expectations, she pushed me, and, oh, I wanted to get an O for Outstanding instead of an S for Satisfactory. My classmates could tie knots, and my siblings would be able to, as well, no big deal. For the remainder of my childhood, this thought drove me. Whether shoelaces or phonics or art, I wanted to do it the same as, if not better than, everyone else.

I was familiar with the verbal tutorial—something about a fox, a rabbit, a tree, and a hole—that was supposed to make the shoe-tying process simpler. But it wasn't a matter of misunderstanding.

It was a matter of strength and focus. Could I hold on long enough, and watch closely enough to prove both sides were capable of working not only independently, but also in tandem, when necessary?

As a young adult, in attempting to achieve so many other day-to-day tasks, I still asked that question. Granted, it wasn't at the forefront of my thinking. I was more inclined to push my limits, and yet I occasionally wondered if my effort was feasible.

I succeeded as a kid. I know, because I also spent time undoing the knot after school, to take off the shoes and align them at the door before going into the house. A Holmes family rule.

I made sure to follow that rule and presently do the same at my own place.

5
SNAP

MY BROTHER EARNED the nickname Snapper, as he loved to snap and frequently did so in his youth. For me, it was a skill that I neither loved, nor did well enough to earn a moniker. And yet it was a big day when I managed to snap with my right hand.

Just as I struggled to allay spasticity when aiming for a shoelace knot, I fought hard to align my middle finger and thumb, and harder still to make them act together to create noise.

In a way, it reminds me of similar steps I took to hold onto the first instrument I desired to play, the violin.

While it proved difficult to grace the fingerboard, and I didn't pursue the skill set long-term, I worked hard to support the bout, tuck the chinrest, and steady the neck.

I occasionally did use my strong hand to situate my right hand. Especially when feeling weak. Even so, I tried to avoid the approach, as it was technically cheating.

Remember, Cerebral Palsy didn't directly impact my left side. So, I easily accomplished any task with that side. But I wanted to adeptly snap with both hands.

On the navy, floral couch in the living room with my mom, I practiced my snap. Shoulder length blonde hair glistening in the light, she leaned over and encouraged me with a kiss atop my head.

"Do you remember what Mary Poppins sang, Joshua?"

"I think so," I said. "What was it again? Sing it for me, mom!"

"Just a spoonful of sugar," said mom.

"A spoonful of sugar?"

"Yes honey. Mary Poppins sang, 'In every job that must be done, there is an element of fun. You find the fun and *snap*, the job's a game'."

"Snap!" I said. "A game!"

"And every task you undertake becomes what? A piece of cake." She then raised and moved her arms like a choir director. "A lark, a spree, it's very clear to see."

"A piece of cake," I said. "Mom, I'm gonna try to snap again."

"And if at first you don't succeed, you what?"

"I know. Try, try again."

Reruns of the NASA explosion quietly flashed in the background on our large, wooden TV.

6
ASSIMILATE

EVEN AS I pushed to quiet my physical deficits, to assimilate into the world like everyone else, I also dealt with regular Petit-Mal (staring) seizures. They were a disruption, yet less abusive back then.

I don't have any distinct memory of seizing at pre-school, perhaps in the grass while running around at the chicken farm and later at the white stone rancher on Lake Road just off of Lake Redmond. Always at the churches we attended, the Red Lion gas station and grocery store, D&K, and the then-Queen Street Bon Ton.

I can't pinpoint an exact day the seizures disappeared, for they didn't totally leave. But it had to have been around my seventh year when a significant change began. There would be a two-year period of occasional seizing.

Constantly outdoors, for recess or leisure, heat and humidity were my biggest causes for concern and precipitators of my auras. Then again, in gym class, trying to play badminton or climb rope, the same factors unnerved me.

The auras affected how I saw and felt the world. Even on Tegretol, Lamictal, among just about every other anticonvulsant, most of my childhood memories include an amorphous perception of my surroundings; In other words, I usually felt I was a part of my own world, but nevertheless vulnerable, merging with a denser, less-contained, nauseating version.

When I merged with this second version, only to temporarily escape it, I also experienced an unexplainable time lapse. Minutes passed even though it felt hours had gone by. And vice versa.

That auras were the pre-cursor to more severe seizures added a layer of angst. I was forced to always be on-guard, to note and avoid all the potential triggers in my environment (i.e. light, noise, motion).

I would see the world through a clearer lens in my late twenties, for longer periods of time after switching from Depakote to Depakote ER, experiencing many of my childhood landmarks undisturbed for the first time.

In my thirties, on Keppra XR and Depakote ER combined, I would go three to five weeks without auras, experiencing the regular world, only to have numerous heavy waves of stimulation overwhelm me, sickening me, hanging a figurative question mark over my life.

I am thankful for my quality of life, but I can still run into the extra-sensory wall at any time.

7
HIATUS

THROUGHOUT MY YOUNG adulthood, I told numerous people of a long-term seizure hiatus. I never tired of seeing the adults' upbeat reactions, the interest, the light in their eyes, the hope for good health.

I remember speaking to a former third grade teacher, a cheery, dark-haired woman, Mrs. Beck.

"How have you been doing lately, Joshua?"

"Pretty good," I said.

"Still drawing?"

I nodded. "Yes ma'am."

"That's just wonderful."

"Guess what?" I said. "I haven't had a seizure in five years!"

"Five years, Joshua! That's a long time!"

"I hope it lasts."

"We all do, Joshua. We don't like those seizures at all."

"No," I agreed.

"They're no fun."

"Not at all."

"I'll think good thoughts for you, dear."

I smiled. "Thanks."

Later though, upon revisiting the timeline of my life, I remembered several instances of seizing. My mother confirmed there was, in fact, a two-year period of improvement before it again changed.

I suppose I prolonged the duration in my mind's eye, to focus on the positives comprising my story. In any event, I had a select number of cases that re-surfaced.

I WAS CLOSE to my siblings in this period.

At Loganville Elementary, my brother, Matt, warded off bullies and somehow daily acquired a collection of NFL team pencils from the school store for me. Later in the day, when auras overcame me in the hallways, I purposefully thrust my body into his classroom doorway, so that he would see and take care of me.

After school hours, my brother, sister and I spent a lot of time together riding bikes. Mine was orange, Matt's was neon green, and Jacque's pink. I had to abstain some days if and when I was too hot and having auras.

Around 1988, we moved to Godfrey Road, into an old, three-story cobblestone farmhouse rental. There, we either spent time in the barn, hunted in the cornfields, or built forts with spare wood behind the shed.

Once, in the cornfield, I had a bad Grand Mal, fell on my back, convulsed in the frosted stalks. I must have gone ahead of my brother and sister and our blonde lab at the time, Hailey, because I came back to consciousness as the dog bathed me in bad breath, soaking my face with kisses, and Matt and Jacque approached. "Here he is!" said Matt. They located me and helped me back to the house.

Another time, at the Spring House just off of our front yard, I seized and fell into the water. We often looked for frogs and lizards there. This time, however, I ran there to retrieve a stray football. To this day, I don't know how long I lay face down or why I didn't violently inhale as I do during many Generalized seizures. My brother pulled me from the water, preserving me again to live another day. Mom then ran to get me.

Needless to say, the hiatus was not what I originally believed. Life unfolded differently than I recalled.

8
TOUGH APPROACH

MY FOURTH GRADE year, I landed in Mrs. Whitenight's homeroom class. The kids called her Mrs. Blacknight because she could be crabby. She was large, had short grey hair, was in her late sixties, was at the end of her career, and, frankly, she frightened me.

Back and forth in the class room, she paced. Clearly ready to retire.

I had heard about her since the start of third grade. I had seen her on cafeteria duty. All I knew was that I didn't want to anger her, and I did my best to follow instructions.

When I first met her, she was rough around the edges, and she mostly established her position by clarifying the repercussions for misbehavior. She was reputed for her tough approach.

She did complete role call, lead the pledge of allegiance, and cover the basic subjects before walking us either to gym, art, or lunch. But it always included a threat of one variety or another.

Seizing regularly, in a different part of the school than my brother, I was forced to rely on Mrs. Whitenight to help me get through them and recover afterwards.

At first, she helped separate me from my classmates, yet still acted aloof. But the more I had seizures and relied on her, the softer and more supportive she became.

I ran around outside once, near the playground, and overheated. I went down in a heap. But Mrs. Whitenight had found a soft spot for me. With a noticeable limp, she crossed the macadam to the grass and sat next to me. She held me for the rest of recess.

I went home and updated my parents on my relationship with Mrs. Whitenight. I honestly couldn't believe the transformation.

"She's like a totally different person, now," I said. "So nice to me!"

"What do you mean, Josh?"

"I don't know. She was scary in the beginning. And then I shook and she took care of me."

"Well, that's a blessing."

"Yeah."

I felt good that, even as a boy, I was able to touch a hardened teacher and see beyond the rough facade.

Mrs. Whitenight was a favorite.

M R. GORE WAS Mrs. Whitenight's friend, and he also frightened me, at first. He was the fifth grade teacher, and he was a proud Corvette owner.

Measuring 6'2" with greying hair and a thick mustache, if he caught you staring into his classroom, he said, "Hey! Yes, you! Stop looking at my class! Or do you want to join us?"

"Oh no," said many kids. "I'm sorry."

"I think you do!"

"Honestly, I don't."

"Just don't do it again."

In reality, though, the kids were just too curious about what happened in the fifth grade, and only a waist-high countertop separated the classrooms on either side. It was hard not to see next door.

While Mr. Gore at first scared me, I also had a similar experience to that which I had with Mrs. Whitenight.

He was initially somewhat disconnected, but the more I seized and the more I relied on him, we grew very close, and he also held me when I took the falls.

One day, he pulled me aside and incentivized working hard.

"If you get an A on the next test, I'll take you for a spin in the 'Vette."

"Oh wow!" I said. "I'll do my best, Mr. Gore."

I was encouraged. A Corvette ride sounded neat! Especially considering my parents owned two loud, Volkswagon Beetles, one blue, one green, and mom used to pick us up in one of them after school.

I had a number of auras and Grand Mals that year, but I also got up again, and I did well academically and artistically.

Before I knew it, Mr. Gore turned into a proud friend. A supportive friend. And as the year progressed, he started thinking about my jump to middle school.

He wanted my transition to be smooth, seizure-free, and he took steps to have me transferred into Mr. Ketterman's class at Dallastown Middle School.

And it would be a smooth jump, as smooth as the Corvette ride that I earned.

9
WHEELBARROW & PUSH UPS

FOR YEARS, my parents did all they could to rehabilitate my right arm and leg, hand and foot. They increased the patterning difficulty.

At different times, I heard them say they wanted to make the process a fun one. And I believe that was their intent. However, I don't recall the workouts as an enjoyable requirement; Perhaps more as a challenge, which I embraced, and at the end of the day is satisfying.

I do remember being a people-pleaser who, during rehab, worked his butt off and tried his very best to make his parents proud.

To this day, after seeing others in York, Pennsylvania with varying degrees of CP, or characters on TV with similar setbacks, I am more than grateful for the steps they took to improve my limb use and lifestyle, whatever their motives.

But the journey wasn't easy. Every night, in fact, for an hour before we could enjoy bowls of ice cream and a good night's rest, I had to complete ten one-armed push-ups in my bedroom, and then walk on my hands through the hallway (dad holding my legs like wheelbarrow handles), down the stairs, back up the stairs, returning utterly exhausted to the bedroom for dessert.

I vividly recall trying to catch my breath, feeling short of it. Laughing. Struggling to carry my weight. The weakness more evident some nights, yet never a reason to quit.

"It's so hard," I said. "It hurts!"

"I know, Josh. But you can do it."

Some nights, we fixated on resistance training, either arm wrestling or moving my legs in circles as if propelling a set of bicycle pedals.

Dad would sit opposite me and count aloud until I had pushed against the pressure for ten seconds, until we both had completed the night's task.

"I can't do anymore, dad," I said. "I can't!"

"Sure you can, buddy," dad said. "You're almost there. And then we'll have a treat."

Regardless of the focus, when finished I always collapsed onto the floor next to my dad, quivering from the exertion. Spastic. An eternal optimist, he applauded my efforts. But it took everything I had to resist the tight tendons in my arms and legs, the burn. It took double the effort from my dominant, left side.

Years of this strengthening eventually developed me in such a way that—while I physically tired more quickly than my siblings and peers—the atrophy was only evident to friends and family, teachers and leaders involved in my day-to-day activities. And even then, many were still unaware of my conditions.

10
ART LEAGUE

WITH THE EXCEPTION of two years, every summer in June I traveled to Huntingdon, Pennsylvania—a small, rural community where my grandparents live—for a week's vacation and art lessons.

Early every morning, my grandma and I loaded the car with our art gear. In the back seat, we placed canvas bags packed with drawing pads and photo reference. In the trunk, we fit the tackle boxes filled with pencils, pastels, brushes, and paint.

We then drove amid the trees, down Cold Springs Road, out to the local Lion's Barn, walked up the stone path to the entrance with our materials, and prepared to create all day with the instructor and about thirty other artsy women.

"I wonder who all will be there," I said. "Any other kids?"

"Many of the regular league members," said grandma. "Perhaps a young visitor later in the week. We'll see."

"I'm excited to get started this year."

"Oh, so am I, sweetheart. We always have such a good time together, don't we?"

I hugged her and gave her a peck on the cheek. "For sure."

The one-room Bingo Hall evoked strong auras every time I entered, the thick smell of paint, turpentine, and bright lights immediately warping my world as so many other locales did. Even so, it was a familiar place; A safe venue in which I honed my abilities, and one that I grew to love.

It took a few years, but the women also embraced me, and as time passed I grew close to several of them.

We all patiently waited our turns to discuss our pieces with the instructor. We also spent many breaks pacing the room, observing each other's work, encouraging and complimenting one another. Later, we ate lunches as a group, outdoors at the pavilion, discussing new art techniques.

Grandma, grandpa, and I spent many more hours talking about art league topics with these same women when we ran into them town, at Sheetz, Original Italian

Pizza (OIP), Michaels, or at church, to name just a few popular places.

Initially, my grandmother joined for leisure. In her prim, box-cut hairstyle, blue denim art shirt, and jeans, she nonchalantly dabbled in the different media as I seriously drew and painted. And even then, she was skilled.

A year in, however, I stopped what I was doing and said, "Grammy, can you please participate more seriously?"

"Oh, your grandma just likes to play around."

"I know. But you are good, grammy," I said. "I'll only continue if you do." I wanted her to enjoy art as I did; To pump out winning works with me.

I won Artist of the Year in third grade, with a linear portrait of Van Gogh that hung in the Loganville Elementary cafeteria for a while. That victory encouraged me to request more of grandma.

From that point on, for twenty plus years until she passed, grandma and I pushed each other, and sought mastery of the art craft.

We had a special connection; An intense one, yet one always lightened by laughter. We both experienced successes and celebrated each other, as she mastered the art of painting, and I mastered the art of pastel.

She and I completed art pieces for numerous competitions and shows, winning awards not only at The Standing Stone Art League, but also at The Huntingdon County Fair in category after category.

Our yearly tradition would mold and refine me into the confident artist and designer that I am today.

11
ROLLER COASTER

THE AMUSEMENT PARK ride at Dorney Park was especially jarring, and at age nine, said my neurologists, its excess movement instigated trauma to my nervous system, provoking the re-emergence of my Grand Mal (shaking) seizures.

It was a hot, summer day. The park was close, assured my parents. And I was in for an amazing time. My brother and sister weren't with us, which meant I would individually experience something special with mom and dad. Little did I know.

As we neared the ride, dad said, "What do you think, Josh? Can you do it, buddy?"

I looked past the line, toward the entry gate. "I think so."

Steel Force was a hulk of a wooden construct that started out harmless, slowly clicked its way to the max height, and then plummeted headlong toward a muddy lake below, only to tilt last minute, circle around and slow to a halt.

It was the largest roller coaster in the country. It still is, thirty years later. But, more notably, and if the doctors' theory is true, it changed the course of my life.

As was the case on so many previous roller coasters, dad sat to my left, and mom to my right. We anticipated a fun time, creating a fond memory.

"Are you afraid?" said dad. "A little bit?"

"Not even a little!"

I was a huge fan of the ride, and of overcoming the ensuing queasy feeling. Perhaps, on some level, defeating the fears of height, speed, and scale played into it as well.

At some point after the drop, though, I started feeling a different kind of sickness. Perhaps a different kind of aura. All I know, for sure, is that I didn't feel well.

The shaking spells didn't occur until days later, but they were bad. Specifically, my first 'new' episode transpired at our second Pennsylvania church, the Gospel Center.

In the next two years, I experienced a lot of violent attacks that were less predictable, appeared worse, and took a larger physical toll on me.

Their origin seemed clear. As time passed, my parents and I agreed the frequent Grand Mals started the day we went to the park.

12
SURGERY

MY PARENTS AND I traveled to every specialist imaginable—from Cleveland to Philly to Pittsburgh to Hershey—in search of answers before settling on a neurology department at Johns Hopkins that claimed I'd make for a good brain surgery candidate.

Famed brain surgeon, Ben Carson, who separated the connected Siamese twins, was supposed to operate on me. As the process unfolded, however, I was assigned Dr. Umatzu, an expert in applying the grid (i.e. a customized brain map) during surgery, who unfortunately died a week after working on me.

I experienced a lot of aura-strewn trips filled with emotion, staying home or leaving school early to keep scheduled appointments, riding on the highways, feeling excited, hopeful, nervous, and uncertain. We had long days in the car, and longer days in the parking garages, cafeterias and waiting rooms.

Said trips preceded a number of predictable clinical recommendations, neurologic assessments, tests, and years of unsuccessful, medicinal experimentation.

We didn't pursue the diet route like we could have, perhaps, but the doctors didn't inform us about it until after the fact, when it was too late. Besides, it was a new trend back then, unproven, and I wouldn't have been excited about changing my meal plan. Generally speaking, we exhausted all options.

I was eleven years old and a quarter of the way through my sixth-grade year at Dallastown Middle School when the surgery was officially scheduled. I still laugh at the fact that I passed sixth grade, having technically only completed a part of it.

I had been training in trumpet at the time, making good progress even though the drugs slowed my processing speed, and it hurt my right finger to cling onto the horn, not to mention my cheeks when I blew. I was proud of the skill set and intended to continue with it when and if I survived surgery.

I had to tell everyone, including my classmates, my school Occupational Therapist (OT), and the trumpet instructor of my pending absence.

It was a lot to ask of someone that age, and I didn't fully grasp what was ahead.

However irrational, I announced it to everyone with a confused sense of pride. Seizures were all I ever knew. I had to be brave! If it worked, I'd be fixed!

My class knew I was a huge Mother Goose and Grim fan, and they bought me a nice, animated, farewell card.

A WEEK PRIOR to surgery, I was admitted to Johns Hopkins. The hospital was huge, but my room was ordinary, institutional, and yellow. A lone TV was mounted in the center, above the bed. I'd remain inside for a month.

My grandma taped a poster with an encouraging Bible verse onto the pale, cinder block wall, including some cartoon character cutouts, which brightened it some.

Friends and family visited pre- and post-op. A church friend, Denny Granville, brought me a copy of *Huck Finn*. The Rowlands brought me a life-sized card with wild animal illustrations.

I first had to go off all my medicine and endure a WADA test, where Phenobarbital (a drug I'm allergic to) and dye was injected into my system, to map out potential motor skill loss and create the grid.

They were most concerned with the removal of my left Temporal, Occipital, and Parietal lobes. It would almost be a full Hemispherectomy, except for the sliver that ran along the central mass of veins.

The second most painful procedure I've experienced, tears streamed at the corners of my eyes, and my shoulders burned as I counted from one hundred, a glass shield encasing my neck, a needle in my groin.

The neurologist sat on top of me when I went into a Grand Mal around number twenty-five, to prevent the needle from breaking inside me.

To make matters worse, that night, upon return to my room, I bit all the way through my tongue. I later acquired a special healing spray from my grandparents' dentist, which helped close the wound.

Until it arrived, though, I feared eating. Swallowing was hard enough, as it was. I had to gingerly place food in the corner crevices of my mouth and consume it with the help of a fluid through a straw.

Still, when I think of the pain I withstood even prior to the official surgery, I can't help but shake my head.

My veins kept collapsing, as well. The phlebotomists tried multiple times, to no avail. Finally, my Aunt Laura— also a doctor—managed to succeed, which resolved one of many issues that exacerbated the trial.

The bright, white lights always on, sleep was hard to come by. The doctors and nurses were in and out, all hours of the day and night, checking my vitals.

Just hours before the surgery, a couple nurses came in and shaved my head clean. All my thick hair gone, they gave me some last-minute reminders, the most vivid of which was the 5 AM wake up call.

In my young life, I had been forced to repeatedly face fears, to leave my parents for MRIs, CAT Scans, and blood tests, but this early morning farewell fell into a fearful category of its own.

At the side of the bed, my mom hugged me and told me she loved me. The nurse had me sign release forms, then said, "You might not see us again."

Two simple thoughts crossed my mind: *If I die, I will go to heaven,* and *If I live, I will have a lot to face with my parents.*

Rolling down the barren hallway, I naively and nervously said, "It's okay. God will be with me."

13
VISION

"JOSH. I'M HERE," said my dad, crying in a void, somewhere to my right. "Can you see me?" I didn't see him. I was alive in the Intensive Care Unit (ICU), but half my world was gone.

It wasn't black, per se; Not even grey. It was just blank, empty, nothing. A terrible loss that still aches today and that I failed to grasp right then. I was scared, and I cried. A piece of me was stolen. And yet I still had to be brave.

Dad leaned further over me, and repeated, "Can you see me now?" I saw a piece of him. The left half.

When I finally saw him in his entirety, I realized his eyes were red and swollen with tears. I reached out to him for a hug.

It is one of those imprinted moments that, my father and I agree, neither of us can erase, and, at different times over the years, we both have relived.

I was in the first recovery stage, dealing with perhaps the worst headache one could have, as the doctors refused painkiller and we later learned I have three veins rather than the usual one in my head.

The way in which they wrapped my head was also problematic. Not only were the bandages tight and painful, enclosing my skull and a collection of connected wires, they itched so badly the medical staff had to tie my hands to the bed rails for fear I might infect the area in question.

It later grew so itchy and painful, the staff removed the first set of bandages, only to replace it with a duplicate set that didn't feel much better but that had to do.

I was in a dark room with full beds lined on either side of me. For thirty-six hours, screaming night and day, I constantly begged to hold onto one of my parents. When they were allowed, they took turns consoling me.

14
SENSE

A S IF LOSING half my sight weren't enough, I also lost half the sense of touch in my body. It was confusing, for I heard the guy down the hall—admitted around the same time for the same thing—had a successful surgery. He apparently hadn't seized since, and came through without a hitch.

I, on the other hand, had a number of hitches to figure. In the days that followed, I placed my hand against the stainless steel bed rails and at the base of my food tray. I learned my left side operated as everyone else's, regularly recognizing hot and cold and reminding me in kind via my assigned pain receptors. After surgery, my right side instead felt a heightened albeit instantaneous sense that left me just as quickly.

How could I gauge pain tolerance and sensitivity, or relate when others hurt, if one part of me detected touch and the other noted a distorted, limited variety?

The last time I cooked on a stove, around age fourteen, I seized and fell atop the burner. My right arm was significantly burned by the time dad found me. And thank God he did.

That said, I was in shock afterwards, tremoring from the injury, leaning against the kitchen island just feet away from the dinner table, and yet I clearly recall a singular sharp jab that told me I'd been singed and then nothing else.

This sensation was similar when, years later, I broke my hand in five places during a seizure. Or every time I twisted back and hit the right side of my head or neck. A shot of excess pain, then nothing.

We were told surgery might result in fifty percent loss of my body, and that it could require an entire year of rehab to get it back. I imagined that potential outcome and struggled to wrap my mind around it. So, in the aftermath, sensory loss seemed small in comparison.

However small, the body does attempt to compensate. I am personally amazed at how my body has adjusted. And yet it takes a personal choice and time to accept the sensory chasm, to grow accustomed.

When you are missing any sense, it complicates things. It influences spatial recognition, perception, personal and physical interaction.

God gave me courage, however, to go out into the world and sense it differently. To create it differently.

15
CATCH UP

BACK AT THE farmhouse, overweight from weeks in bed, my head still crusty after several cleanings, my face swollen and eyes still lightly bruised, I tried to catch up on the school work that accrued when I was gone.

Stepping beyond the hospital walls, back into reality, it seemed a lifetime had passed, that everything I now knew was suspended in slow motion—slower than slow motion, actually—and everything around me was flying by as if nothing had happened to me.

But something *had* happened to me. My seizures actually changed; evolved, so to speak. I had less predictable auras, stronger Grand Mals that seemed immune to treatment.

I also banged into nearly everything now! If it wasn't a cabinet, a closing door, it was a wall. In public, if it wasn't another person, a shopping cart, it was a car mirror.

I had to learn how and where to look, wait, walk, sit, and stand all over again; On the right side of the world if at all possible, but on the left and in the middle too, when the option wasn't readily available. I felt foolish and angry about this, unjustly punished, and even yelled at and kicked a few chairs and car tires afterwards.

I also recall feeling fragile, especially sluggish. My medicine already offered that side effect, and yet, mentally and physically, I initially worked through what reminds me today of heavy cold symptomology.

I was eager to jump back into my pre-op life. The one that evoked excess attention, but far less than what came from the botched surgery. I wanted to feel normal. As much as I could. I mean, I *had* survived.

On different Sunday mornings, the Huntingdon Alliance Church and Grace Fellowship Church asked me to stand and publicly acknowledged my survival. Everybody clapped, and it was incredible to see the thrill.

Even so, my entire family and I wanted to return to pre-surgery normalcy. But we did have a set of medical instructions to first abide by.

I stayed home a few weeks before delving in. My head was still healing. My energy levels still growing. My coping capacity still expanding.

Before the school work, though, I had to catch up on opening gifts and reading through well wishes. The Dallastown teachers sent a fruit basket with cards. Numerous church members were also kind enough to offer encouragement in notes, books and artwork.

There was plenty of transitional support. Pre-made dinners. Babysitting. I can't refute that. And yet, inevitably, the entire ordeal delayed me, emotionally, physically, developmentally. Some major changes occurred and exacerbated the delay when I returned to school.

At Dallastown Middle School I had to daily dodge trouble, the 'no-hats inside' policy, showing my shaved head and scar, explaining to teachers why I wore a baseball cap as a cover in the hallways. And then, even after dad fought to get me into the class, the trumpet instructor forced me to quit because, in her opinion, I was too slow and too far behind to catch up.

The tone of the classroom changed too. And not for the better. Mr. Ketterman was unhappy with his position, as he wanted to coach football instead. And my peers hadn't been taught how to accommodate a classmate dealing with loss. They didn't know how to talk to or treat me. So, I was often isolated.

Many days, I preferred a different isolated place; The bus to think, a lone bathroom stall, or perhaps my home in the country.

My family and I lived at the farmhouse rental for the remainder of that year. And like so many others, summer came and went.

Dad had his eye set on the one-acre plot of land across the street where he'd build the clay, Cape Cod in which I'd live and adjust for the rest of my high school years.

16
JUMP

THE JUMP FROM the farmhouse to the Cape Cod across the street was officially our fifth move, but technically the first big family adjustment since my surgery. It was hardly the last. In fact, in a transitional sense and a literal sense, I remembered a number of other jumps I participated in with my brother while living at our new home.

Nineteen ninety one to 1995, Matt and I were still close. Best buds, I'd say. We shared the same bedroom and bathroom for years. Cycled through a love for different sports, even though I enjoyed them from a distance. He was fiercely loyal. That's how it always had been.

Up until one day my freshman year, when he came home consumed by music, no longer interested in fort building, in hanging out. We did everything together. And then we just stopped, taking separate paths.

It took some getting used to, but I eventually accepted that Matt made new friends, that things changed. That not everyone stuck to the same routine. That everyone moved on, and liked different things.

Our community was small and took its time developing, so, while Matt's shift seemed sudden, time still unfolded slowly on Godfrey Road. I still rode bikes and played outside with neighbors.

I continued to live life occupied with being a good Christian and son, with avoiding seizures, completing homework on time, and, now more than ever, improving in my artistic endeavors.

I thought about our other jumps when I was alone.

"ARE YOU SURE, Matt?" I said to my brother on an especially hot, isolated day in 1992. The second jump I recalled. A year had passed since we made the move from the farmhouse to the Cape Cod. I was fully recovered from surgery, had lost the excess weight, regained my strength, and was back to enjoying country living. "I don't know about this idea."

As a whole, in an effort to grow a thick mess of grass, the Holmes family unearthed an incredible number of rocks from our new piece of property, an obscene amount every Saturday really, and yet digging a ten-foot square hole on the side of our house? It didn't seem so logical.

We had mown that lawn, run around the yard, thrown baseball and frisbee, kicked soccer ball and football, decorated a garden with grandpa, even identified a place in the woods to build forts, but never had we constructed a hot tub.

"Sure I'm sure, Josh! Would you stop worrying so much and just start digging?"

I looked at my shovel, paused, wondered if I could do it, and then, foot to the metal, jammed it into the earth. I was feeling nervous and starting to have auras.

Mom and dad had taken a week-long trip to the Caribbean, and Matt was convinced they would love a surprise, homemade hot tub. For some reason, I couldn't imagine my parents appreciating it.

Didn't hot tubs have tile-covered basins? Chlorinated water?

I might have agreed with Matt had there not been so much mud. But each hour, we stood a foot deeper in our yard, absolutely caked in dirt. It grew more and more difficult to push out and dump the wheelbarrow at our wood line, too. My auras grew more intense, but I endured.

I was twelve and Matt was ten. And if there was one thing at that age worse than disappointing mom and dad, it was disappointing my brother.

And so, against my better judgment, I dug with all my might, through southern Pennsylvania's infamous red sod. The random smells of public bathroom should have tipped me off.

I will say that, as the hours passed, and the half of the hole that I could see seemed more uniform, my auras settled, and I thought, *Well, maybe they'll like it. It does look a little more professional now.*

"It does look better," I conceded.

"Just wait until we fill it with water."

Matt and I unwound the long, green hose mounted out back and pulled it around the side of the house. After another several hours, we managed to fill the entire hole with muddy water, although it did seem to quickly evaporate.

MOM AND DAD pulled into the driveway, and I thought, *Oh boy. Here we go. I sure hope they're happy.*

Matt led them through the front yard and to the new hot tub.

"We built you guys a hot tub, you see?"

"You dug all this?" said dad. "Oh wow."

"So you can soak and relax."

"It was Matt's idea," I said. "But I helped."

Dad ran over to the sand mound, a mix of disbelief and concern etched on his face. He caught a whiff of sewage and scrunched up his nose. "That was very kind of you, but the septic tank, boys. We could have had a mess on our hands!"

"But it was a sweet thought," said mom.

"Where is all the dirt?" said dad.

"We dumped it back there," I said, the auras in my eyes again flaring.

"Boys, we'll need to fill that in right away. Before it rains."

My body ached. And the thought of refilling that hole after an entire day of creating it? Overwhelming. But I knew it was coming.

I worked my tail off filling in the hole that evening, trying to rectify the situation. I felt weak in my right side, but I wanted to fix our yard.

The experience taught me two things: I learned that good intentions didn't always justify my actions.

And I learned to think twice before jumping at my brother's next prompt.

M ATT WAS ESPECIALLY convincing, though. A gift he still has today. I recall thinking twice the winter of 1994, yet ultimately jumping into another situation I would never forget.

"It'll be so fun, Josh," said Matt. "Come on, you'll love it!"

Our next-door neighbor bulldozed a valley for privacy, and built his house sideways. That is, he pointed his garage and front door eastward. He was nice enough. But dad had told us not to go on his property.

Even so, a beautiful snow had fallen. School had been cancelled, and we had a thick bed of white before us, just waiting to be packed and ridden upon.

Staring at the hill that dipped past our property line and into our neighbor's open, cement foundation, I again said to my brother, "Are you sure?"

I was now fourteen, Matt a more confident twelve.

Decisively, he tightened his grip on the front of our long, orange sled. He told me to do the same, so I held firm in the rear. With that, we started the fast slide, leveled out for a moment, and soon after breached the foundation.

In mid air, two things happened: Matt had the wherewithal to realize how high we were and jump out of the sled, and I froze, falling ten feet, ultimately connecting with the basement floor, putting three ribs out of place.

Instantaneously, the air was sucked out of me. I struggled to inhale, due to the pain in my side.

In immediate protective mode, Matt pulled me from the snow-strewn sled, put his arm around me and assisted me from the basement and valley.

"Why didn't you jump?"

"I just didn't think," I said with a whimper. "I know I should've. But I didn't."

"I can't believe it!"

"I know."

"We need to get help."

Fortunately, Dad met us halfway. At our mailbox, actually. And after a quick check up and admonishment, he called Kurt Bauer, a close friend and chiropractor from church. Dad explained the situation, and soon after I was at ChiroCenter, on my back, arms crossed, getting re-aligned.

OFTEN WENT to my new room—the former guest bedroom at the top of the stairs—and locked the door to either read or listen to music after school, to sleep off post-seizure migraines, or generally to keep to myself.

Due to differences, I asked to move out of Matt's room and into my own. The guest room already had a bed stand and a bookshelf, so I was set. My parents saw the need and permitted me to do so.

After 1995, I watched Matt and Jacque attend school together. It seemed as though they grew closer and they jumped into personal and social activities. But perhaps not as much as I originally thought, my sister later clarified.

In any case, they were around sometimes, and away other times.

Because I lived with constant medical issues, I wasn't your typical teen. At least insofar as my general attitude toward jumping into new things; Especially those that I knew were off limits. I just didn't desire them.

And so, while I remembered my early jumps with Matt, humorous and naive though they were, I stayed focused on God, art, and school, and instead jumped alongside Christ to pave the way for my future.

17
FEW FRIENDS

THE FACT OF the matter is that the unknown typically frightens people. Difference, in general, can as well. People often exaggerate it, and then either isolate or embrace it.

My conditions over the years have presented many with the opportunity to ignore me or welcome me. And I have experienced both tendencies, within and beyond the church setting.

While epilepsy, partial blindness, and Cerebral Palsy didn't initiate a negative response at home, in public they evoked horror and disbelief from everyone.

As the years went by, they also instigated regular liability fears, as everyone seemed more concerned about getting sued over my sudden falls and injuries.

Police officers, EMTs, and everyday observers fought over me—at bowling alleys, movie theatres, restaurants, and football games—as I lay there, my speech gone, my body lifeless, hearing and seeing everything, but waiting for my faculties to return.

It wasn't a once and done thing. I saw it everywhere I left my mark, so to speak. If I could count the number of free tickets, coupons, and discounts I accrued from fearful managers and owners.

After a while, the whole idea of going out lost its appeal. I had to function as everyone else, and yet the chances of making a scene, of horrifying someone, of inviting fear were strong. I grew afraid of frightening others, and I had no say over it.

I'm already an introvert. And yet, over time, I grew claustrophobic and withdrawn.

I DID HAVE reference, though; Memories of friends who, despite personal concerns, looked past my conditions and treated me as an able-bodied person, as someone they valued.

The first was my quiet yet strong, Filipino-American friend, Marissa Kline-Gonzales, who in middle school took care of me many times, preserved my head, following my seizures, when all of my other classmates refused to help. She didn't have to, but she knew what it was like to need help, and she was there to offer a hand.

In the gym, once, I felt overcome by auras, the echoes of basketballs and teen argument fueling the attack. Certain I was going to have a Grand Mal, I tried to get to a safe place away from the court. I called out to Marissa. I fell, but she caught me and cradled my head in her lap until I returned.

When I was back to myself, we carried on as friends, conversed and played basketball after school, putting aside my malady for the time being.

In high school, my affable buddy, Andrew Baker, a tall, dark-haired kid, was that friend. Both artists, we shared a bond, had good times in art class, in choir.

I didn't see him while he went to college, but we ran into each other in 2004, while I lived in my current complex, York Apartments. We spent a lot of our free time together. And, like Marissa, he too would help me in my helpless state.

The most memorable instances for me occurred during and after a Dave Matthews Band concert. I received concert tickets as birthday gifts for years, and it was my thirteenth time to attend the event.

Thousands of people at the Hershey Park Arena, the jazz instruments blaring through the nearby speakers, Dave strumming and singing, I had auras throughout, which eventually turned into a Grand Mal.

Andrew held me while on the ground until my seizure finished. People flipped out, as was the norm. Once my legs and arms worked again, he then helped me beneath the bleachers, beyond the tarps, where the EMTs looked me over and eventually released me.

Our wild night continued, as I fell into another episode on the road home. To keep me off the steering wheel, Andrew had to extend an arm and ward off my shaking body as he also tried to drive.

Tail lights flared ahead of me. Car lights streaked past me. Entangled in my seat belt, I struggled. Afterwards, I couldn't breathe, like usual. Delirious. Parched. Beyond exhausted.

Late at night, he managed to keep his cool and descend Hershey. A couple hours later, he got us back to York.

I could tell countless similar stories, mention nice people who assisted along the way, but the point is: My friends cared for me in my time of need.

Regardless of how others treated me, I knew how they ought to.

18
HALF & HALF

AS OPPOSED TO my previous drawing style, where I saw everything and simply blocked in all shapes on one hundred percent of the page, after surgery I had to adopt a different method, where I sketched in the half that I could see, and then moved over the matboard and completed the other half.

Instead of assigning all the color at once, I added to what was in sight, and then filled in the rest as I moved to the other side.

I learned, with practice, the significance of anticipation in the absence of sight. How could I traditionally address the unseen? Well, I couldn't. Faith, however, offered a different perspective.

While I didn't immediately know what was to unfold on the page, I had to trust the new process. And with each increase in scale, this fact became more evident. What a change in approach and style!

In many cases, I'd complete the majority of a picture that looked fine on the left side and distorted to an extent on the right. It was bound to happen. A perfectionist, however, I refused to rely on the notion of artistic liberty and continued addressing the defects.

As I established, I had few close friends; Marissa in middle school, Andrew in high school. This is still the case, although my network has drastically grown.

My brother and sister had their own set of extra-curricular activities; Basketball and soccer and music for Matt; Theatre and dance for Jacque. And once they each could drive, they were never around. Our relationships changed.

As such, I had a lot of free alone time to visit and re-visit drawings, to examine disproportionate halves, and learn new ways to work around my deficits.

Sitting on a sheet to contain chalk dust, my pastel and pencil boxes open and in a row, I listened to hours of 910 talk radio in the background. Here and there, I added and subtracted, blended, fixed and refined.

A chalk piece raised to the drawings, vertically, then diagonally, I judged space and angle, criticizing every minute discrepancy.

During the Penn State sponsorship commercials, I turned off the overhead light, and I stepped away, to affirm perspective and analyze tone from a distance.

It could be frustrating, but I had the drive to defeat imperfection. My parents and grandparents pushed me hard, too. So, I had plenty of reasons to find answers.

Red Lion Christian didn't offer challenging art classes during my middle school years, grades seven through nine. They did offer an interesting Shop class, which taught me how to weld and solder. But art? No. I continued drawing outside of school, learned more, and produced several high-quality pieces.

By the time I started Christian School of York in 1996, as a tenth grader, I was so proficient I jumped into the advanced art classes. I shared the same classroom with Andrew, but I began Art Two, for select juniors and seniors, a year early, an accomplishment I always felt proud about.

19
HUNTINGDON SWIM

ART WAS MY love, and defeating my visual cut was a worthy challenge, but, as my fellow artists could attest, I had to take a break from my creative space every now and again in order to easily return to it.

That said, I visited grammy and gramps, members of an electric co-op, at nearby hotels and restaurants in Harrisburg and McConnelstown, every chance I could, after which they'd sometimes return home and spoil me for a week at their place.

On one such occasion, my grandma took me swimming, to do something different, mind you, only to watch me fall into an episode.

Without hesitation, she dove in the Detwiler pool to save me. I was fifteen years old, in the deep end, in mid-aura, quickly falling into a Generalized seizure.

Water had always been my enemy. Ever since the Spring House incident. I loved to swim, but, growing up, my parents had to join me so that I didn't seize and go under.

After a boy drowned just feet away one day in a public pool, mom and dad were even more careful.

Later, when hungry for more independence, I wore a life preserver. A vest was a requirement at the beach. And while I initially felt embarrassed because I stood out, I eventually acquired a sharp, neon ensemble, and learned to appreciate it, for I had an enhanced ability to ride the waves.

But not this day. In a haze, I waded to the corner of the pool. I had the wherewithal to hold onto the side. The water levitated like a crystal blue escalator, and the concrete pad felt as if it was morphing into the water.

The sound of crashing waves slapping the pool tile walls echoed around me. In my trance, I observed my grandma slice through the pool like an Olympic athlete.

"I'm coming," she said. "Just hold onto the side."

My speech left me, and my head started turning, as it always does during a Generalized seizure.

"I'm almost there. Just hang tight."

Released from the grips of the seizure, I slowly turned forward again. I slowly soaked things up, that time warp feeling encapsulating me.

In blouse and slacks, grandma waded through the deep end, until she reached me. Her traditional, box-cut askew, she finger-brushed her hair aside and grabbed my hand.

"Are you okay?" she asked. "You gave your grammy a scare!"

"I'm okay. Just disoriented now," I said. "I'm sorry."

"Don't say sorry. You didn't do anything wrong."

We moved along the wall until we arrived at the shallow end. We then pushed through the water at our waists until we at last came to the stairs.

20
DRIVING LESSON

I DIDN'T ACQUIRE a driving license like my siblings and peers, thereby gaining that desired adolescent freedom. Nor did I get a first car and set of keys, a highlight for many teens. Despite my scary experiences in water, I did, however, manage a unique driving experience with my gramps on Lake Raystown.

My grandpa was an avid outdoorsman, upbeat and always on the go. Next to God, his wife, his kids, and his grandkids, he most loved navigating the woods and the water.

He owned a silver fishing boat with a number of seats and a double motor that afforded him a means to traverse the water and anchor as he pleased, to cast and reel his rod for fish.

As a general rule, he kept it parked outside his home, by the dog house. When ready, he hooked it up to his truck and hauled it to the docks roughly forty minutes away.

Back in the day, grandma and I would set aside the artwork and meet gramps at the lake, sometimes for lunch; Other times, we came with food and soda to refill his Igloo. Later, I accompanied grandpa alone, enjoying longer afternoons together in nature.

My epilepsy, limited sight, and skewed sense all kept me from riding the roads and highways. It was illegal for someone with seizures to drive, unless there was a year of absence and proof of medical control. So, I typically rode as a passenger.

I rode as a passenger on the silver boat, as well. Until one sunny day, grandpa turned away from the boat's steering wheel, and looked back at me, strong and serene.

"Would you like to drive, Josh?"

The thought of swift movement frightened me. The swaying motion atop choppy waves stirred enough stimulation as it was.

"I don't know gramps," I said. "Is it safe?"

"Sure, it's safe!"

Technology at the time hadn't advanced to the point of present-day drones and automated vehicles. While concerned, the thought of manning a sixteen-foot boat also excited me, and I felt it was the *big* opportunity.

"It would be the closest I'm ever going to get to driving."

"The lake isn't busy today, Josh," said gramps, throwing his arm wide. "You see buddy? All clear. You'll love it!"

I wasn't sure. But it was a chance to know the feeling of driving.

"Alright," I said. "I'll try it. But not too fast."

My dad once had me sit on his lap and steer his car in the church parking lot. Later, my friend Marissa allowed me to steer her dad's truck in a parking lot, but I basically circled a few parking spots and that was it. Steering the boat for miles seemed a step up, more demanding of all my senses.

Grandpa and I traded seats. I situated myself behind the walkthrough windshield. There was an open expanse ahead, and while I couldn't see everything, I settled into my new role as captain.

"You want to go faster?" said grandpa. "You still have plenty of room."

I hesitated again, but quickly decided to take the risk. Grandpa demonstrated how to shift the throttle. Soon the wind gusts tightly grabbed us, the hull of the boat raised, and it bounced off the water like a kite catching a jumpy draft.

For a couple miles, we rode at this pace. There were a few boats in the distance; Woods everywhere; Off to the side, the Raystown Lodge, where we celebrated my grandparents' fiftieth anniversary one year.

Before long, however, I grew comfortable with the speed increase. I did wonder how similar a car drive might be, if I could operate it the same way and avoid feeling flustered. Would I instead grow nervous, indecisive, and crash? It was hard to say.

For now, though, I was on the water, enjoying my time with gramps. "You're doing great buddy! If you want to crank it up some more just push the throttle like I showed you."

And so, one final time, I increased the speed. The steady airstream clawed at my dark hair. My eyes leaked. I didn't have a care in the world. Under the right circumstances, I could see how one might love the feeling of total independence offered on the water.

We covered the full length of Raystown Lake, before finally turning back, and docking for the evening. It was an exhausting trip, for sure. All that sun and gale force in my face! It was not my typical routine, and yet it was especially exhilarating.

21
OVERTIME

THE CONCEPT OF working overtime was ingrained in me early, and was reinforced in high school, long before I worked a full-time job.

When I wasn't in chapel, refining my art (the yearly art show always at the back of my mind), or awkwardly engaging with my peers, hanging with Andrew, I was always playing catch up and tutoring, to comprehend what easily clicked for everyone else.

I was a good student. A responsible student. English was always easy for me, and I loved it. With all the sensory and medicinal interference, however, school, in general, was a struggle. Even so, I went out of my way to stay on top of everything.

Perhaps the most demanding subject that required academic overtime was math. I tried so hard, and still I received several disappointing homework grades. I felt sick and perplexed, until one day—when I realized I was in trouble—I decided to address it.

"Mrs. Packard," I said. "Do you have a minute?"

A sweet, elderly woman with a perfect perm and a wealth of knowledge, my teacher said, "Yes dear. What is it?"

I looked at my homework paper, the bad grade in my hand. "This is the sixth bad score in a row! I need help."

"Yes. You are struggling, dear."

"So what should I do? I can't keep this up."

"I told the class I'm available to those with questions. And I would be happy to tutor you, Joshua, but it will have to be over the lunch hour."

"Thank you, Mrs. Packard," I said. "I want to get this, so I'll be here."

"Good for you, young man."

For two years, outside of class, I practiced Algebra and Geometry with Mrs. Packard.

She spent her time smacking chalk against the green board, drilling the fraction, decimal, and cross-multiplication techniques into me. I attempted to complete the unfinished problems on the board and also took practice tests, which she looked over and corrected.

On test days, I lingered over break to finish what I didn't get done during class. Mrs. Packard knew I tried hard, and she allowed me the extra time to complete everything.

I wanted to hang out with my peers over lunch. Instead, I rushed my meal, and I stood at the island in the front of the classroom, scanning over the problems as quickly as my eyes would allow, answering the ones I knew, guessing the ones I didn't.

There were some days when I still worked on material, next to the steep stack of completed tests, even as the next class ambled in after lunch. The demand for speed made me nervous, and the auras persisted.

I quietly lay my test on Mrs. Packard's desk, and then I ran to the next class, hoping I didn't get called out for it or have to publicly explain the delay.

I got a B in Algebra, and a C+ in Geometry. I wasn't thrilled with the grades, yet I was satisfied I passed because of the overtime work I put in.

Looking back, I see how I applied that same overtime sacrifice again and again in my collegiate and post-collegiate careers.

22
GOLDEN CHARIOT

S TILL AT SCHOOL, the CSY secretary, Mrs. Shelley, named the wheelchair the "Golden Chariot" as a joke. To lighten the mood for my classmates, I guess, after having watched me seize hard on the ground. Perhaps she was trying to make it less embarrassing.

The name—a spiritual reference to Elijah's unique mode of transport to heaven—tickled her. She chuckled at her own quip. It secretly bothered me, because my transport to the windowless, nurse's office was anything but fiery and heavenly.

It always involved an inquiry about whether or not I'd taken my anticonvulsants, why I thought the seizures happened that day, and if I knew of my mother's/father's plans for the day or of their whereabouts so that we could make contact.

Whether she picked me up in English, Science, Bible, or Typing class, all within close proximity to one another, it always seemed to occur the same way.

The teachers, afraid, would take a moment to convince themselves everything was ok, attempt to act unfazed, and then they'd face the students.

But I shook there, a spectacle next to and beneath the desks, and gasped until it was all over.

"Can I have two strong young men," asked the teacher. "To come and help?"

"I will," said the bully who had just picked on me that morning.

"I'm coming," said another.

"Everyone else, hold hands in a circle around Joshua."

My body was dead, and I was barely awake. Enough so, though, to watch and hear the school bullies lead the entire class in prayer over me, and then assist in lifting me.

In my stupor, even those who regularly mistreated me participated, primarily acting out of fear yet under the guise of religion. The hypocrisy ate at me some days.

Still experiencing auras, I then would spend the school afternoon alone in that small side room until mom or dad picked me up.

So many school days I spent in that isolated room!

23
TIPPED BUS

THE SECOND TIME I made the newspaper was another local "Against the Odds" piece, but even more so a confirmation that God was watching out for me.

I realized He'd done so during surgery and every seizure instance, but the Grand Mals were constant thorns, and I never desired to reflect on how much deeper they could lodge in my flesh.

The fire and brimstone sin messages of Red Lion Christian and watered-down doctrine of Christian School of York deeply impacted me. They made me imagine an angry, performance-driven God.

I often wondered if I'd done something wrong to deserve my afflictions, causing me to feel debilitated, hopeless, and carry unnecessary guilt.

The day my big yellow bus tipped over, however, offered a visual opportunity to note what could have happened, what didn't happen because of His mercy.

It was a typical rainy day, the skies murky, the air humid and unsettled; Another long bus ride home, one of many we'd taken throughout our high school years. My friend Marissa, my brother, sister, and I were the only ones left for our driver, Jeff, to drop off.

As we slowly passed over the white bridge and rounded Grayden Road, though, Jeff lost control of the bus. The front wheel latched onto a patch of moist grass at the top of a deep embankment.

Jeff briefly looked back at us. "Guys. Girls. Hold on. I think we're going over."

It all happened in an instant. I attempted to grab onto the back of a seat, to say a prayer. Before I knew it, however, I was in mid-air, under gravity's death grip, and then connecting, shoulder first, with the roof.

I do remember wondering whether the bus would tip over and stop on its side, or if, on the slope, it would roll, tumbling all the way to the wood line, possibly going up in flames. Considering the hill and size of the vehicle, the latter seemed more likely.

And yet, shoulder against the roof, all was still, and I felt relatively unscathed, perhaps bruised. We did need to get out of there before the bus decided to move.

"I think it's over, guys," said Jeff, half-turned, counting heads.

"Everyone alright?"

"I am," said Matt.

"I think so," said Jacque.

"Me too," said Marissa.

I sniffed the air, a slight tinge of gas lingering in my nostrils. I looked at the seats below us; At the shards of glass spewed all over.

I then touched my shoulder to see if I missed any injury. "So am I," I said. "I'm pretty sure."

"Okay then," said Jeff. "Let's carefully try to get to the rear exit."

And so, my brother used the fire extinguisher to break open the Emergency door in the back. We all crawled out the opening, and Matt ran a distance to the nearest trailer, to call for help.

My parents and a reporter showed soon after. Perhaps a cop or two, and a service to haul away the fallen bus. As severe as the accident could have been, it didn't attract much attention beyond that.

My siblings and I assured our parents that we were unharmed, and then we offered statements for the front-page article to come.

I was blessed that day.

24
FUTURE PLANS

SHARED WITH my classmates the story of the tipped bus and how I had been spared. I thought it would more than surprise my peers.

Perhaps it might even help me fit in. Other than Matt, Jacque, and Marissa, who else could claim such an accident? Such a miracle?

I brought in the newspaper clipping to school. Over the next week, I saw a wide array of reactions. Some expressed disbelief. Some expressed relief. Beyond that, though, the rest either minimized it or showed little interest.

A lot had transpired in our Senior year: The Senior dinner, The Senior trip, The Senior prom. Meanwhile, my seizures and neurology consults continued outside of school. I had to consider and decide upon different treatment possibilities.

What most weighed on our minds was graduation night. Performing with the choir before the walk. Accepting the honors. And for me, the teacher announcing my future plans to the entire audience.

We practiced the formal ceremony in the gymnasium that afternoon, so that we knew how it should play out for our friends and family that evening. It took a few runs, but by all appearances, it seemed as though everyone in attendance would enjoy the spectacle.

If you went around the room, you'd see that we had a classroom comprised of young men and women who would pursue a vocational spectrum. We had the pastors, the teachers, the manual laborers, the collegians, the non-collegians, and the artists.

As an artist that consistently put out new work, it was evident that art was my area of expertise. Even up until the final week, however, I still hadn't decided whether or not I'd pursue fine art, architecture, or graphic design after high school.

I took a drafting class my Senior year to see how well I'd handle technical drawing and deadlines. I made it through the class with a C, but spasticity in my right side and time crunches ultimately impacted my work quality.

I also took a tour of the local design school, The Bradley Academy, which was a reputable school yet far from the larger fine art schools (e.g. The Cleveland Institute of Art, which I was interested in and that accepted me). It also required a degree of technical artistry I feared I didn't have.

Nevertheless, I knew my buddy Andrew would be headed to Drexel for Graphic Design. A couple other creatives announced similar directions. I knew that, no matter my concern, I had to take the stage and own my future.

I still had time. We first had to sing the three songs for the crowd. We performed the classical pieces on cramped bleachers, only to return to our rows in the audience. Our choir teacher thought they were hits, nodded in approval afterwards, and I would receive a number of compliments for the arrangements later on.

That night, I stood in the shadow at the base of the podium. I shuffled from foot to foot, nervously, and watched as twenty students took their turns before me. After fifteen minutes, I inhaled and climbed the stairs.

I slowly made my way toward the principal and a teacher, who both were also dressed in their formal gowns. The first handed me my diploma, and the second placed my Deans List rope around my neck.

It was finally my time. I bowed my head in thanks, and then turned to step up to the lectern. I smiled as mom whistled, dad yelled, and the crowd applauded.

When the silence settled in, I listened to the speakers crackle, and then a third teacher stoically announce what was also documented in the school program.

"Joshua Holmes, Class of 1998, plans to attend The Bradley Academy for the Visual Arts. He will major in Graphic Design."

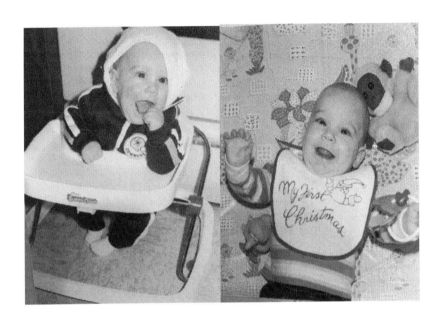

When the tires of this Dallastown Area School District bus rolled off the pavement, they slid on wet grass and the bus, with four students inside, soon tipped over. No one was injured.

DAILY RECORD / BIL BOWDEN

PART TWO

College Life

1998-2007

25
IMPLANT

THE SURGEONS LATER placed four Vagus Nerve Stimulator (VNS) devices inside of me, at different times between the ages of seventeen and twenty-six.

The implant was a small pacemaker for my brain inserted under my clavicle, its case hard in my chest and its wire tightly wrapped around the Vagus nerve in my neck.

The surgery left me feeling as if someone had punched through my chest and twisted a fist left and right, back and forth, sucking the air out of me every time I moved.

Theoretically, it was supposed to offset excess electricity in my head by shooting an opposite charge every two minutes for thirty seconds.

A separate, corresponding magnet that I could carry with me had the power to negate the charge, if an instance ever required it.

My parents and I had the side effects talk beforehand.

"We know that it might change your voice," said mom.

"Yep. It might alter my tenor," I said.

"And it could involve some level of discomfort," said dad.

"Nothing else has worked," I said. "So it is worth a try."

"They've worked for a lot of people," said dad.

The trick, as is the universal and rarely-achieved medical goal, was to find the "therapeutic level" of charge. I'd heard that reference when dealing with medication. It was important when weighing chemicals, but it was even more so when measuring the electricity that coursed through me.

And it proved to be harder than they thought. Nineteen ninety-eight was a whirlwind; My first year of college at the Bradley Academy for the Visual Arts. A Graphic Design major, I endured a year of intolerable yanking, tugging, and random neck pulls before the doctors landed the correct settings.

I synonymously fought the multiple side effects of an anticonvulsant, named Topamax. It exacerbated the damage done to my neck, toyed with my mind, elevated my body temperature, and made me so sick I wasted hundreds of dollars on food that originally smelled good and then later repulsed me. I lost twenty-five pounds by the time I got off of it.

AROUND THE SAME time, I was hit by a car. Well, the driver ran over my foot and I somehow broke his windshield before falling to the ground.

The school day was over, and like most days, I was feeling sick, eager to return home, running distracted across the street to my apartment. Out of nowhere, a vehicle emerged.

I still remember the second before the connect. And I marvel at my instinctual reaction, despite the blind spot. Dare I call it miraculous?

Like an upper-level karate block, I raised my arm to my forehead before penetrating the glass. I hit hard, but I don't remember a surface buckle or crack. My art bag flew from my shoulder.

I also remember the weight of the tire on top of my Doc Martens. The wheel indented the outer shell of my leather shoe and pressed into my left instep.

The head blow didn't negatively affect me, thank God. And besides temporary discomfort, my foot was also unharmed.

For the second time in my life, though, someone thought I had died. The driver and his wife got out of the car, frantically talking in a Middle-Eastern tongue, and started chanting and dancing over me.

I opened my eyes, first squinting at the sky, and then glancing at the dancers. I didn't recognize their moves.

It took a moment, but they realized I was alive and then calmed.

We later discovered that they were my neighbors. They approached my father about the car damage. With so much happening, dad settled it out of court, his insurance paying a portion to quietly resolve the matter.

I LEFT THE Bradley Academy before the end of the year. I didn't finish the Design program, even after Dad advocated for me. Primarily because of my CP, sickness, and emotional state. But, once free of crippling VNS settings and of Topamax, I put it behind me and transferred to Edinboro University of Pennsylvania, ready to start over.

Edinboro University had a great art program and was renowned for its disability services. The school accommodated hundreds of persons with disabilities, including me.

Those needing round the clock care benefitted from special on-campus housing. Others, like me, lived in reserved, first floor dorm rooms. I also had access to the Office for Students with Disabilities (OSD), which availed me of extra testing time and on- and off-campus transportation.

I became close friends with all the drivers. They cheerfully took me from point A to point B, shared good stories, and made memorable conversation. They all had good hearts, and each went out of their way to improve my experience.

I also met and befriended numerous people with CP, Paraplegia, Quadriplegia, deafness and blindness en-route to class and even on the way to grocery shop.

They all were after a degree, integrated into the school, in every major and minor.

I majored in Fine Art and minored in English. On my second implant and a different mix of anticonvulsants, in a new, snowy environment, I continued to experience constant auras and had numerous Grand Mals. My processing speed was less than stellar, and my grades suffered.

With time, the device offered a sense of psychological support, but there was no proof that it physically helped, that it decreased seizure activity. There was no indication that it improved my lifestyle or academic performance.

Nevertheless, I was an academic at heart and a fighter. I pushed ahead, even though my second attempt at a college career looked bleak.

Near Edinboro, the town, I found an active, growing church, called McClain, that sustained me with solid Christian teaching. It also had good worship, and a twenty plus singles ministry that offered a number of events and travel amenities. It was independent and by-the-book, yet it helped me spiritually and socially, and ultimately honed my focus on God and school.

I attended weekly with my Christian friend, Marla Brumbaugh, a sweet, sensitive Education major from Pittsburgh who helped people with multiple conditions on campus and who wasn't put off by my seizures. After church, we then dined at the cafeteria.

On the way home, I found myself singing the worship songs I heard at McClain. I then recalled, one Sunday, seeing that choir was an optional elective.

My implant still jolting me and vibrating my vocal chords, I soon after tried out for the school choir. At the piano next to my choir teacher, Dr. Vandenhonert, I belted out a few chords on key. Deemed a bass, I joined the group, of which I was a part, and with whom I performed for four consecutive years.

One of my favorite Christmas memories is performing on stage at a small church in Pittsburgh, seeing my parents, grandparents, and great grandma enjoying the Hallelujah Chorus, proudly applauding out in the audience.

Despite the fact that my voice always changed, I was proud of my membership, and loved singing, representing my university at schools, churches, and retirement facilities all along the Eastern Coast.

After two years of Fine Art, I met with my advisor, looked at my completed core classes and electives, and switched my major to English and my minor to Writing.

The VNS implant settings and medicine the same, I managed to master the writing craft, salvage my GPA, and in 2004 earn my first Bachelor of Arts (B.A.).

26
COURTHOUSE

THE ROUGHEST PART of York City looked a little rougher each morning I rode the Red Rabbit fixed route to the courthouse. It felt a little more foreboding too, darker and decayed, as my auras were especially strong then.

I lived alone at the York Apartments complex, in a first-floor unit on Brentwood Drive. It was in a safer area, but I was cognizant of my surroundings, and of how we all could live in an unrealistic world, assuming safety where it wasn't.

Once the crime-ridden section was behind me, I entered the brighter part of the city. I stopped for a quick iced coffee at McDonalds, and made the daily trek down N. George Street. Caffeinated, I then jogged up the steps, passed through security, and into the halls of justice.

If you had asked me what I would do following five years of collegiate Art and English and Literature study at Edinboro University of Pennsylvania, I would have said "Whatever the Lord wills," and probably "Something in journalism, I imagine." Never "Oh, probably clerking at the local Criminal Courts office." But in 2004, that's exactly what I did.

For months I'd applied to different writing outlets, online institutions and even the same local newspaper I'd made twice. Opportunities were few, however. Despite natural talent, I lacked substantial experience.

Walking in public one day, I ran into Don O'Shell, an old church acquaintance who in my youth briefly taught me the soundboard. In passing, I mentioned my job search. As the acting York City Clerk of Courts, he told me of a temporary opening in his office.

The courthouse was another place with unique energy. The excitement was two-fold: The building was not only crawling with criminals and anxious families, but it also was brimming with officers, lawyers, judges and clerks seeking just results.

Even so, I saw the majority of it through a cloud of auras. The place was full of varying wavelengths and white lights, which enhanced the extra-sensory experience.

Responsible for hundreds of documented criminal charges and cases, and mail delivery, in a small way, I contributed daily to the overall operation of the legal system.

I still hear the clerks saying to me, "Folder open. Expungements on the left. All other documents on the right. Make sure they're filed in order."

Like most office jobs, I always had a new stack of files to prepare, input, and store away. After a rushed lunch at the Central Market, and an afternoon of minimizing the load, I settled on an acceptable stopping point.

I then either walked three streets to the hub and took the bus home, again passing the morbid part of town, or hopped a ride with my mother.

For the duration of my courthouse employment, I entered demographic data, delivered packages, and witnessed courtroom hearings; Specifically, I observed an intriguing and informative three-day arson case. After which, off the record, the defense attorney asked my opinion not only of his client's verdict, but also of his tactic to present family members as character witnesses. And I opined that the prosecution's case convinced me of guilt.

The clerks were territorial and competitive, and the office morale was lacking. Nevertheless, a part of me hoped Don would have the funds to prolong my stay.

But the funds didn't show. Upon completing my work, I inevitably had to decide where I would go from there. It was an uncertain time.

The big question was: More school or more interviewing?

A long time Penn State fan and dreamer of higher education, after many prayers I decided to visit State College, to pursue a scholarship and Masters Degree (M.Ed.) in Counselor Education with a Rehabilitation focus.

27
INTERVIEW DAY

COUNTING THE DAYS to the State College trip, I was cautiously optimistic. I even smiled to myself when I considered it all. Inside, though, I was a mix of emotions. Filled with a healthy sense of pride that I was going. A healthy sense of joy that life was moving ahead. And a healthy fear of my competition and the interview. I did believe and say, "If it's meant to be, it will be."

But, deep down, I wanted it perhaps more than anything I'd wanted in quite a while. A Masters from Penn State! I had gone through all the motions. I sent in the application with numerous demographic, personal history and personal philosophy questions to the school. I waited. And subsequently, I received the invitation letter.

For weeks afterwards, in preparation at my apartment, I went over a handful of common interview questions, I worked on selling myself, on my body language and sharing my disability story with confidence, on setting myself apart.

I remembered sitting on the floor as a boy before a large TV in Huntingdon, watching the Nittany Lions football team play in the National Championship, and enjoying the school spirit so much that I dreamed of attending the university one day. And now I was preparing to go to main campus and gain entrance into the Rehabilitation Counseling program. I had to present as an asset to the College of Education.

The big day was a sunny Saturday. I was dressed up in my finest interview attire: a white button down, black slacks, a grey tweed suit coat and tie. Mom and dad also donned formal garb, as we were going to meet and greet at the famous Nittany Hotel before the staff panel called me back.

Once we arrived, I found the suite hosting the event and loitered in the lobby just outside. The department had three silver trays of cheese, crackers, fruit, veggies and dip spread out on a table. On the other side, the department secretary guarded the spread of pre-made nametags for those of us visiting.

The auras strengthened as I approached the nametag table.

The secretary looked up at me. I told her my name, she handed me a packet, and sifted through the plastic. "Joshua Holmes? For the Rehab Counseling Program?"

"Yes. Thank you."

"The staff introductions will start in a few minutes," she said. "Over there. Until then, enjoy the appetizers."

"I think I will," I said. "I appreciate it."

There was a different kind of energy in the room, an energy laced with confidence but also with competition and hope. The fifty candidates knew they were a select few, and yet they hadn't officially finished the protocols or qualified.

It was just so new to me that I felt overcome and eager to see things transpire and watch where God was ultimately going to take this.

I grabbed a muffin and ate it in a nearby corner out of the way.

I shook a few professors' hands.

The formal introductions filled me with even more excitement, but with repeated silent prayers, I contained myself and projected confidence until it was my turn.

"BEFORE I BEGIN," I said. "I can only see half of you, so if I don't respond, or respond late, I'm not ignoring you. I just didn't see you."

Dr. Herbert, a warm, bearded man and Dr. Mpofu, an equally warm clean-shaven man, greeted me, and then walked across the humid room to their chairs. They settled in with intrigued expressions on their faces.

I reminded myself that they'd already conducted the same interview multiple times, likely in the same way, before I walked into their assigned room.

I strolled to the chair nearest the door, the only one left, and sat erect, looking straight at them. "Just to avoid any miscommunication, you understand."

"Yes Joshua," said Dr. Herbert. "Thank you for that."

I anticipated a long conference table to separate us. Instead, thirty feet of open space united us.

"I'm excited to be here. Thank you for the invitation."

"So Joshua," said Dr. Mpofu, momentarily standing, tossing his suit coat over the back of his chair, and again sitting. "As you know, we have invited a number of candidates. Only twelve will be chosen."

"Yes. I understand."

Dr. Herbert unbuttoned his collar. "In fact, we will only hand out twelve scholarships for the fall class."

"Yes."

"Tell us why we should pick you for the Rehab Counseling program?"

A hollow stream of aura ran through me and I took a subtle breath. They seemed more relaxed now that they had set aside the jacket and loosened the collar, but they were still hungry for a substantive response.

"To be honest," I finally said. "I think I would be a great candidate. I've been a Penn State fan since I was a kid. It would be a dream come true to study here."

Dr. Herbert listened, and then wrote on a tablet and nodded.

"But more than that, you guys know I have a number of disabilities, that I have thrived my whole life with them. For five years, I lived with and assisted numerous friends with disabilities in Edinboro. And I believe I can relate with the disability community perhaps better than anyone. Training here at Penn State would test and refine my existing skills."

Dr. Mpofu smiled.

"Also, the ultimate goal is to work for The Office of Vocational Rehabilitation. I've been an OVR recipient for years. Worked with them a long time. I understand the process. So I believe I would be a welcome addition to your program."

They both turned to each other. "Anything else, Dr. Mpofu?"

Dr. Herbert cocked his head and lifted his pen to the air. "The program will involve hours of open discussion and writing. How do you feel about that?"

"Again, I think I would benefit the school. I not only did both in my undergraduate English program, I entered hundreds of criminal cases into the computer in my time at the courthouse."

Dr. Mpofu whispered in Dr. Herbert's ear. They each then nodded in agreement.

I sat there, nervous, purposefully animated. *Whispers. A good sign? Or one of disinterest?*

"Well Joshua, that will be all for now. It was a pleasure speaking with you."

"And I with you."

"When we have made our final decision, we will be in touch."

28
DIRECT OR INDIRECT

"JOSH, YOU JUST aren't asking the right questions," said Ava, the dark-haired, Indian Ph.D student evaluating my practicum interview session. "So many direct, closed questions!"

We sat in one of the closet-sized counseling rooms. The scheduled evaluation occurred after my counseling sessions, after Ava's own classes, the cameras on the walls documenting our exchange.

Somewhere along the line, in my twenties I picked up a tendency to ask 'yes' and 'no' questions. I didn't ask open questions, those that would ultimately allow me to learn about my client and accrue information for a final goal.

At least not yet.

Ava crossed her legs and grimaced.

I was on the tail end of my first year of grad school. I was thrilled to be accepted, got through the first semester without a problem, was pleasantly surprised by the challenge posed by the Masters program, but I ran into a roadblock in semester two.

"You aren't applying Reflection of Feeling, either," said Ava, placing hands atop her knee. "The client has to know you understand what she is feeling."

I cocked my head. "She gets that I understand."

"Does she now?" said Ava. "How do you know?"

"Well she is still showing up, isn't she?"

"Yes, Josh. But I'm not seeing enough progress."

"What about there?" I said, pointing at the video unfolding on the TV before us. "That was a good summary."

"Not as empathic as it could be."

"So, I'll ask questions with more feeling and empathy."

"You've been saying that a while now."

To pass the Doctoral program I knew she had to impose another level of criticism, regardless of accuracy. So I reminded her of this. "I've improved, Ava."

"Your questions can't be so harsh."

Sometimes, the sessions felt forced. Or came to an abrupt halt. The inquiries didn't come to me as fast as I wished they would. So I knew there was room to improve.

I thought with more effort Ava would declare me empathic enough, but our meetings seemed to repeat themselves, and in the end she submitted my evaluation marked in red.

"I will be speaking with Dr. Hunt."

At my advisor and professor's demand, I subsequently sat through a heavy grilling of my current status in the program, as documented in the Doctoral report. It was an emotional meeting that had me in heavy aura. But I left that day, resolved to continue.

Before long, I was answering to my professor. It was embarrassing that I was one of only a couple required to complete practicum under such scrutiny.

But twice a week I abided by the parameters placed on me, and my once harsh approach came around. By the time I was finished analyzing my counseling sessions, I grasped the sensitive method they expected, and I applied it to my newly-assigned clients.

The caveat I had to accept was that I would get a C for practicum, not good enough to pass, and I would have to take it again the following year. It was devastating, and yet I held my head high and pushed on.

My sweet, red-headed friend and colleague, Anne Keller, and the rest of the girls in my class were there when I came from Dr. Hunt's office every week. They offered some much-needed support.

29
KARATE BASICS

I N THE YEAR leading up to brain surgery, 1990, I not only took trumpet lessons, but I also took karate lessons. My dad and I studied at Kim's Karate in Red Lion, Pennsylvania, Tang Soo Do, only to have the Sensei take away my opportunity, because of the operation and subsequent missed time.

Eleven at the time, I was introduced to the basics of the Martial Arts, the kicks, punches, blocks, and kata. We saw a decrease in seizure activity, and even as a boy I loved the study.

I was intrigued by the requirements, and more so to see my body adapt and do what everybody else's did.

And yet I wouldn't return to it until 2005, the start of graduate school. I avoided athletics and physically-demanding group activity for many years. Part of it was fear of inability. Part of it was fear of peer/leader response. Part of it was logistics.

That is, until State College availed me of a place that offered a means to address all three.

Five blocks from my apartment at White Course resided a tiny pizza shop with a hidden gym out back. I walked by it every day on my way home.

I saw a generic sign advertising Jiu Jitsu and Kali classes. Excited, I reviewed my schedule, planned to visit the gym and inquire about cost.

A WHOOSH OF hot air slammed me in the face the evening I looked into the gym. *No air conditioning*, I thought.

At the entrance, there was an office; In the center, there was a mobile boxing ring; To the left, there was a weight room and a staircase that led to an upstairs loft.

Members yelled, weights clanked, and bells rang as I turned into the front office. Sporting a dark ponytail and a tank top, the owner/boxing trainer sat behind an old desk.

"Hi there," I said, stepping into the doorway. "I am interested in your Jiu Jitsu class."

The man pointed to the loft. "They are fifty a month, and a new class begins next week."

"Sounds great!" I said.

The man pulled at his ponytail. "It's not for the faint of heart."

"I have plenty of heart," I said. "And I can't wait."

Thai Jiu Jitsu, specifically the wrist bending and required over, under, back hand movements (also known as an uchi uke in Japanese), did wonders to re-train my brain. It helped me efficiently use both sides at separate times, laying the groundwork for Kali, stick fighting.

Once muscle memory was established, in the steaming loft my instructor led us in hand-to-hand combat, shin fighting, and stick manipulation.

My karate partner and I practiced with bamboo sticks. The contact not only helped build an immunity to pain, but also secured a tolerance threshold.

Every Tuesday and Thursday, after stick sparring, I walked home feeling alive, adrenaline-laced. I was dehydrated, bruised up and down my arms, thighs and calves. And yet I felt prouder and more accomplished than I did completing any academic assignment.

Group class was a challenge, as it always required integration, self-imposed or not. The belt-free system, where the novices learned from the veterans and vice versa, made it less hierarchical yet easier to fall behind.

There came a point, when I felt—in order to step it up—I needed one-on-one lessons. I needed to address my deficient ambidexterity and strength.

For the duration of my personal lessons, my Kali instructor, a young athletic guy with a buzz-cut, focused on my right side, returning to some of my childhood warm ups, and having me twist heavy, industrial metal rods. It hurt, to put it mildly.

And I worked at this, even as I carried a full-time class load, participated in lengthy class debate, and balanced paper after paper. I persisted while daily eating with and coaching the kids of Lifelink PSU, a transitional support group for teens with disabilities.

Despite constant aura, I made it through all the karate classes without enduring a Grand Mal. I saw the loft through that all-encompassing, amorphous lens, nevertheless I pushed the limits.

Physically speaking, perhaps the greatest things I took from the experience were: The degree to which I warded off my CP, and the improved dexterity in my right limbs. More than ever, I could not only twist but, if necessary, also sustain a stationary position.

30
UNEXPECTED TURN

J UMPING AHEAD TO 2006. Two years into the three-
year Rehabilitation Counseling Masters program at
Penn State University in State College, Pennsylvania.

I loved Happy Valley. The energy and school pride
were unmistakable; the exciting vibe emanated throughout the college town. All around, there was just so much
to do!

I had some of the best years of my life there, between
attending football games and concerts, studying the
Martial Arts, hanging with my friend and fellow counselor, Anne, and helping people in general.

I also loved visiting with my grandparents nearly every weekend, dining out at The Waffle Shop and The Outback, shopping at Target, Dick's, Sam's and the mall.

Every year, I looked forward to the State College Arts Fest, which was an artist's paradise. I'd heard if I was ever accepted as a vendor, it would change my artistic standing.

On and off campus, one could see acres and streets of tents housing different prints and products. My grandparents and I spent hours talking with artists and perusing artwork for sale. My parents met up with us one year. Afterwards, I was always inspired.

But again, 2006 took an unexpected turn. My schedule was full, so when I had a chance, I made an effort to get home. On break, I rode the Amtrak train into Harrisburg, where my parents picked me up and drove me back to York.

As was the norm for several years, my parents and I planned to return to Harrisburg a few days later, to support and watch my brother, Matt, perform with his rock band, Sinclarity.

We were roughly halfway there when, all of the sudden, my implant started jolting me so strongly, the pain was unbearable. I couldn't breathe.

In the back seat, I desperately grabbed at my neck; The battery juice leaked in excess. I hacked and choked, trying to clear my throat.

"Something's wrong," I cried. "I can't breathe!"

Mom remembered we brought the magnet I hadn't touched in all the years of owning the implant. That seemed to be a God thing, after the fact.

I held the magnet to my chest for several minutes, and the electrical jolts slowed, yet not entirely.

"I'm pulling over!" said dad, turning into McDonalds.

They ran in and got me an orange beverage, I attempted to drink it, but with each charge, the drink foamed at the back of my throat and came back up. I threw it up all over the parking lot.

I still held the magnet to my chest, but with each movement, I was jolted hard again.

Dad ran to the trunk and came back with duct tape. I held the magnet in place, and he wrapped the entire roll around my chest and back until everything was secured in place and the jolts decreased even more.

Needless to say, we wouldn't see Matt's concert. We all got back in the car, made an emergency call to my surgeon, and immediately returned to York.

At midnight, my surgeon met with us at his office and turned off the device battery. The next morning, I had it taken out for the last time.

31
IN SESSION

MY PROFESSOR WARNED me about viewing the video documenting my seizure. "You shouldn't watch this one," she said before me in the hallway. "It was bad."

But I didn't listen. I thought I could handle seeing myself shake and cry. Even in session.

"It's alright, Dr. Hunt," I said. "I'll do it."

"Josh." She looked harder at me. "I'm serious."

Appreciatively, I nodded. "I know. Thanks for the heads up."

I was in my final year of graduate school, completing my second counseling practicum in the Penn State University Cedar Clinic, a small, outdated reception area with a note-taking room, and a cluster of connected interview rooms. I'd met with and counseled a lot of troubled clients there.

A new group of graduate counseling students had been recruited, and my friend Anne and I were the only two of my original class still remaining, working again in the clinic to refine the Rogerian, person-centered counseling skills adopted by the school.

The task was challenging, but after the critical first year assessment and 2006 implant malfunction, I didn't think anything could rattle me. I still dealt with stomach damage, still treated it. Little did I know, though, how painful the recorded session would be.

For months, I'd been watching and transcribing my sessions. After hours of listening, questioning, reflecting, and summarizing client issues, I then spent several more hours staring at a VHS TV monitor, wearing headphones, typing as fast as I could.

Afterwards, I typically handed in my notes, my transcriptions, walked across campus, over the N. Atherton bridge, and headed home to White Course, where at least one of the three International graduate students with whom I shared the quad loitered inside.

Some nights, I ate at the dining hall, and then found a place in The Stacks at the Patee-Paterno Library to study or write. Other nights, I studied with my female colleagues in the Kern Graduate Building café.

On those nights that tested my endurance, I reflected on one of two highlights: Either my acceptance letter or Orientation Day.

The acceptance letter arrived in the mail on a Sunday morning. My hands trembled as I pulled it from my mailbox. *Is it possible my interview was solid enough?* I thought. *Just be prepared, regardless.* The packet included a letter that stated, "We are happy to inform you that you have been formally selected to join the College of Education." There were some coupons for a few free on-campus meals, and a lanyard for my PSU ID. The cirrus clouds danced away, and the blue sky seemed to grow bluer. I was filled with a deep gratitude and said, "Thank you Lord."

My parents were on their way to get me for church. Standing in the sun, I could barely handle the good news and couldn't wait to share it with them. A day to remember, for sure.

If I needed to dwell a little longer, I re-lived Orientation Day. All my peers and I participated in a survivalist camp. We each had to rely on one another to make it to the next obstacle and complete every station. When we defeated the challenges as a group, we then earned a piece of the long, green rope used on the course.

"You will face considerable challenges in the next few years," said Dr. Herbert that day. "May you hold onto this piece of rope and may it represent a promise to finish what you started."

I held onto it. And they were right. I faced a lot.

This night was different, though. A higher level of challenge. For the first time in my life as an outside observer,

I saw my condition wreak havoc. I struggled to type as I watched myself fall forward out of my seat, land on my client's lap, get up, walk in circles around her, making a high-pitched noise.

I saw a person that wasn't me. And yet there I was. Under a spell. In an event I didn't remember. Like an out-of-body experience. *Why?* I wondered.

My client said, "What are you doing, Josh? Stop it!"

"Please," I said. "Please."

She then realized I wasn't right. She ran out of the room for help and never came back.

We were making progress too. In our third session, I was facilitating a better meeting, asking better questions, and seeing better results. She was opening up. Then I seized and that was it.

A deep sickness settled in my gut for the rest of the week. It was devastating. Doubt gnawed at me. *Am I pursuing the right field?* I wondered. *Should I continue?*

THAT SUNDAY I walked into the same State College Baptist Church I had attended for the past three years. It was a plain white structure with aluminum exterior paneling, and a set of double doors that opened into a hidden yet authentic, safe space.

The physical stomach ache and sickening devastation in my gut still lingered, but I knew the Spirit filled this place. And if I was to continue, He would make it possible.

While attending the church, I was introduced to the Apostolic world, to signs and wonders and healing. I'd grown up in Fundamentalist schools and Independent

Mega churches. I was used to required norms and pre-defined order.

As a teen, I'd participated in grandiose Easter musicals for years at Grace Fellowship in York, which was an entertaining ministry. My parents, siblings, and I sang and acted on stage. The tongues, dancing, aisle-running, and flag waving in the audience, though, was quite a change.

I had experienced moments of healing in this service where I was certain I could see the whole picture, my world broader and brighter. To gauge my perception, I'd sit forward and move my eyes from side to side. Granted, it returned to my normal half-world when I walked outside.

Perhaps the most impressive part, though, was the worship. It was upbeat, free-flowing, and genuine. I had never yet gone to a church that spoke to me more through music than through teaching. I experienced it alone, and when I attended with my Trinidadian friend, Isaac Dialsingh. I often found myself reflecting on the phenomenon.

In the second pew, I asked God to touch me. I prayed for peace and strength. I asked Him to heal my stomach ailments. I allowed the instrumentation and lyrics to wash over me, and I quietly cried.

The needed, supernatural relief filled me. The physical and emotional pain moved on. And I walked out, ready to leave behind the past and to embrace the future.

I finished the program strong, weekly representing my class, contributing to the department Climate Committee, writing a thirty-page thesis on the deaf and hard of hearing communities, completing an internship with *CareerLink*, finally earning a second degree, my graduate diploma in December of 2007.

PART THREE

Work and More

2008-2013

32
CLOSED DOOR

WITHIN A FEW months of graduation from Penn State, I was hired in Philadelphia for my first official Pennsylvania state counseling job. It was my last choice, but I had unsuccessfully interviewed everywhere else.

The graduate scholarship was contingent on immediate employment, so there was a lot of pressure to land available Civil Service openings. I made cold calls every day. I scored well on the test, was high on the list, and yet my physical conditions complicated the job acquisition process.

The Office of Vocational Rehabilitation (OVR) had financially assisted me in every one of my academic efforts, had provided tutors, had bought me computers, and even supported my pursuit of a job with their office.

They claimed their focus was facilitation of persons with disabilities. Some even called me an OVR poster boy. But when the time came, when, in the interview room, I requested accommodation for my epilepsy, eyes, and CP, I lost the job offer every time.

It was surprising, too, for in the counseling field, there was a heavy emphasis on acceptance, multiculturalism and diversity.

The Philly office was my fifteenth interview try, but it would be my final attempt. After hours of practice, I said the right things, properly answered the questions, and adequately expressed interest.

M Y FIRST WEEK in Philadelphia, I lived in a hotel, *Days Inn* on 4th Street, while my apartment was prepared two streets over. Sunday night, I watched Super Bowl XLII in the hotel lobby. The Giants against the Patriots. Afterwards, I had some time to get acquainted with the city.

Betsy Ross's house stood a block away, and, starting nearby, the colonial Old City spread out over eight blocks, statues and instillations creatively aligned below Main Street.

By January of 2008, I'd moved into my new apartment, and I was situated and carrying a caseload of three hundred people.

I attended state gatherings and visited local schools. I completed every necessary protocol. I got along with everyone. By all appearances, everything was alright. But it quickly changed.

I was supposed to place thirty clients in jobs by year's end. I landed a few clients in training programs, a couple in jobs, but not at the rate my supervisors wanted. I struggled to keep up. I created the paper trails they desired on the required system, but there was always a problem, even when I thought I'd done well.

Every month, I received negative evaluations, as if they decided my plight from the very get go. If it wasn't my case notes, it was my humor, my gait, my tone, my performance.

Many nights, emotionally raw, I hung out with my co-worker and buddy, Jason Signor. He was well aware of my situation and could better relate with me because of a different albeit similar visual impairment.

"Jason, I just don't get it!" I said. "It's like I can't do anything right!"

"I know. It stinks."

"So, what should I do? Did you see what Rose did to me today?"

"Yeah, Josh," said Jason. "I just don't know."

We would then let it go. After a brief pause, we changed course; Walked and talked and joked all over Philly. The city bustled. We tried out new restaurants, my favorite called Pizzacato, took the L train to the 8th Street Station, and even bowled once or twice.

If unavailable, I walked home alone to my loft on 2nd Street and either wrote or drew. I penned several novel scenes and pumped out a number of beautiful art pieces. I started what would turn into a pastel series of musicians that I later showcased and currently hang over dad's Grand Piano in his music room.

I COULD HAVE used some comforting background music the night I had a seizure on the L train, on 2nd Street, and awoke all the way down on 35th Street. Instead, I heard the automated female voice announce, "Doors are closing."

I was seated on the floor, angled against a foldaway seat and my head lay in my arms like a teen taking a nap in class.

I didn't recall going into the seizure. I didn't remember the people around me. And I didn't grasp the time that had passed.

I was shocked that my bag was still next to me. Someone lay me in this position and was kind enough to leave my belongings be.

It dawned on me that I had to immediately get off the westbound L train if I was to catch the return trip.

Only the day before, I traveled to 35th Street for the first time. I was visiting a training facility for clients. Looking back, though, it seemed a God thing, and I was grateful I came to consciousness on a street with which I was loosely familiar.

I gathered my things and, last minute, caught the door. I then ran over to the nearest SEPTA coin collector. "I just had a seizure. Woke up a minute ago. I'm kinda disoriented. I need to get back to 2nd Street."

The sound of shrieking brakes filled the grotto. The noise grew louder as the eastbound L train approached.

"Ok hon," said the coin collector. "Here comes the eastbound. You'll want to hop on and take it all the way back to Old City."

I N MY OFF time, parading through the streets and the subways, I met and befriended several homeless men and women.

Every few blocks, a person sat against a fire hydrant, holding a sign claiming victimhood, requesting money. And between those blocks, the more brazen homeless just approached and point blank asked for money.

Still an OVR employee, I felt convicted to share my business card with the homeless, and I always invited them to the office and promised to place them in a job or training program. I sometimes invited them to church. They typically vowed to try, and yet I never saw them beyond their perch.

I first met Frank, a kind, round, fiftyish African American man, underground, who gladly gave me directions and encouragement as I waited for my ride.

I found out that he lived on the PNC Bank window-sill on 4th Street, and I stopped by many mornings and evenings to check on him. I also invited him to visit me at work and church, but he was most concerned about avoiding the cops.

Frank went on to introduce me to many of the regulars. He took me to South Street and 7th Street and 10th

Street, introduced me to the homeless men and women who claimed the given street.

"George was in the war. I don't know how he'll act," said Frank. "Deep down, though, he's a good guy."

"Ok," I said. "I'll be quiet."

"And Judy? Been out here for twenty years. She's not going anywhere soon. You'll like her."

And, surprisingly, I did like her. I liked most of them. But breaking the street-loitering habit was not a part of my role. As much as I wanted them in a home of their own. Friendship was my role.

Toward the end, I decided to use my offering to feed Frank and the gang. I informed them all I would not hand over cash but told them I'd treat them to breakfast or lunch.

My parents and grandparents told me to be careful but supported my choice to feed the less fortunate.

Frank and I enjoyed Nick's Roast Beef on 2nd Street. He remembered visiting the restaurant and meeting Nick in his youth and made the experience a memorable one.

MY EMPLOYER EXTENDED the six-month trial work period for another six months. I continued on, doing my very best, even though it was clear my supervisors intended to fire me as soon as possible.

Every day, I walked out of the elevator, signed in, entered the bland office, and passed through the maze of dizzying cubicles all around, the smell of sandy, industrial carpet squares in my nose, straight to my own cubicle, in hopes of avoiding a new issue.

Every part of me wanted to quit. This job was not what they initially advertised. They wanted my counselor credential, period. In truth, the counseling was minimal. The data collection and entry were excessive, and, bottom line, it entailed processes too chaotic for my taste. Nevertheless, I persisted to the end.

I attended the famous Christ Church on some weekends for encouragement and sustenance. I desperately needed it. It was a beautiful place, architecturally speaking. While logistically convenient and community-oriented, I didn't experience the joy and peace I knew at the State College Baptist Church.

So, I did visit other churches, to connect with a group. In the meantime, Jason—also a believer—supported me as my career devolved and his flourished. We hung out at each other's apartments, watched TV, and speculated about our futures.

His friendship did help me to endure. He was able to explain procedures I misunderstood, give me insight into office goings-on, and offer advice on how to handle situations.

As I tried to apply his advice, I also took weeks of documented mistreatment to the Union rep, and even rode the L train all the way to 36th Street and handed it in at the Governor's office. It upset both parties but amounted to little else.

The entire ordeal was incredibly painful, and yet it was necessary to welcome in God's entirely different, better direction.

33
OPENED WINDOW

FORMERLY THE BRADLEY Academy, The Art Institute of York, Pennsylvania presented as a place of function: Compact, abstract, and orderly.

"Follow me," said the petite, dark-haired, admissions rep. "We can talk here."

She shook my hand, and then led me past the front stairwell, the art gallery, through the right hallway, straight back to her office.

Now experienced, I gave a solid interview and asked relevant questions. I mentioned my disabilities but didn't spend a lot of time on them. She didn't see them as a problem.

Once settled, she glanced at my art portfolio, my previous transcripts and GPA. "An impressive body of work, here, Joshua," she said. "And great grades too. You should be able to start right away." Immediately, she accepted me into the Graphic Design A.S. program.

UNHAPPILY LIVED in my parents' basement for several months after the firing, uncertain about my life direction, again drawing downstairs alone, listening to talk radio, before I finally resolved to look at my God-given talent, art, as a possible career avenue.

I actually applied to, submitted an online portfolio to, and later visited Towson University, interested in their five-year MFA program. And I was impressed.

Meanwhile, I considered the Art Institute. It had changed some, and yet it was still that familiar, first academic locale I attended as a teen.

It was not your traditional state university, Edinboro University of Pennsylvania for example, which I started nearly ten years prior. AI York was small, trade-based, accredited, and operated under the guidance of numerous teaching professionals.

They offered the core classes and required electives. Nothing more, nothing less. Ultimately, the school was meant to prepare its students for design positions.

This final fact resonated with me.

I T WAS IN this same timeframe that I tried the anticon-vulsant, Vimpat. Since Topamax, I hadn't consumed a seizure drug with such sickening and scary side effects.

To this point, I had accepted the doctors' suggested drug experimentation. It was tiring to start a popular pill, increase intake, only to get 'weaned off' when it didn't work. And yet it had been my treatment approach and was a part of identifying a fix. But Vimpat changed my perspective.

I earlier explained the two worlds I enter and escape during aura. The time lapses. Vimpat made me feel as if I'd stepped much further into the second dense world, and question whether or not I could exit. Time seemed an illusory figment, the light so bright inside, my nausea compounded tenfold.

My heart knocked in my chest, a hammer, like never before. Up to the moment the aura felt it would turn Generalized. Only it never did. Until some undetermined future juncture.

Following the initial spell, an aura-free period ensued. But, on Vimpat, it guaranteed the second aura with a Grand Mal to come. One I couldn't remember.

As was the case the day I resolved to walk from my parents home to Giant several miles away. I knew it wasn't wise, as Vimpat could draw me into that world on a dime. But I was independent, and I refused to allow a drug to steal my freedom.

A brisk autumn afternoon, I trekked halfway down Chestnut Hill Road before diagonally cutting across a soggy cornfield that nearly sucked off my shoes. I made it to Springwood Road, though, and continued through the yards of some older homes.

But that was when woods emerged on either side, and the berms narrowed. My eyesight the way it was, it felt as if I had entered a broad tunnel that restricted with each step.

An angst festered inside me. The Vimpat auras again pulled me in, the deep light blinding me. I walked to the left berm. *Please help me, God*, I thought. *I screwed up.* And then it all went black.

I awoke on the right side of the road, in the clearing of a wooded residence. I was perplexed at how I ended on the opposite side of the road, frightened and angry that I couldn't even take a walk. And yet I was grateful for the supernatural protection.

The homeowners were watching after me, when—of all people passing by—my mother came upon the scene. I later thought, *You just can't make this stuff up!*

Once again, The Lord preserved me. Man, oh man, I had to get off this drug.

I N 2009, MY life made a full circle and returned me to the very school circumstance forced me to abandon in 1998. Yes, I was fired in Philly. Yes, I had to go through some things while at my parents' house. But I had another chance to re-try a former life stage. I still say to myself, "How can anyone deny God's hand in my life?"

The Towson interview didn't go my way, and so I completed the steps to transition at the Art Institute of York. Financial Aid. Orientation. Shortly after, I moved into AI York campus housing and started my third college experience.

By this time, I'd spent so many hours honing my fine art skills, I had adopted a personal style and was adept at duplicating just about every image I tried.

Graphic Design, however, demanded all the skills that reside on the left side of the brain, which I had removed during surgery.

Granted, over time, my right side had compensated. Nevertheless, I had to conquer skills that involved numbers, measurement, precision, and software savvy. I didn't realize what a challenge this would pose, but I found out pretty quickly.

34
QUAD

JUST AS I lived in a quad (a four-room apartment) in State College, I did the same at the Art Institute. With the exception of John, a talented animation major who lived with me for all three years, new students cycled in and out each spring and fall.

So far, I had lived with guys from Japan, China, Korea, Australia, Puerto Rico, and Trinidad. On some level, even when we had occasional tiffs, The Lord availed me of opportunities to show His love, to discuss Christianity with them all, which I was glad about.

The designers and artists that lived with me at AI York were a different breed than those graduate and doctoral types at Penn State. For one, they were much younger. For another, they were inexperienced. A part of God's Plan, I presume, several dealt with varying degrees of disability.

I no longer helped as a transitional coach or worked as an official counselor, and yet in the apartment I had to listen to and advise young men with a host of mental health issues, ranging from depression and autism, to paranoia and schizophrenia. There was always something going on.

Per one parent's request, I actually awakened a student for class when he grew overwhelmed. Another, I calmed when he had visual hallucinations.

The majority of the students in my quad didn't complete the programs, due to the severity of their cases. As an individual with medical conditions, however, I was able to speak with them about their current attempts and situations.

FOUND MY third karate class opportunity attending a different church one Sunday. For the three years I went to the Art Institute of York, in an effort to build my faith and better equip my struggling housemates, I visited The Upper Room, a charismatic church with a nice congregation and a very analytical pastor.

When I needed a change of pace, a lighter sermon, and a different worship set, however, I walked to Connection Christian Church, which was equally nice and resided just opposite The Galleria Mall food court.

Its exterior reminded me of an ultra-modern bank; Square in places, steep and angular at the center. I don't recall if I heard an announcement or saw a sign, but I asked about the class.

And sure enough, free Tae Kwon Do classes were offered twice a week in the back room, a spacious area with wooden corner closets, hard and matted floors. I thought, *That would be cool to train again while going to school.*

The Lord knew of the years I didn't participate in sports, knew my heart, and as such provided ten-fold in adult opportunity.

Master Mike Winter, the dark-haired instructor, was a tough, kind guy. A black belt, he led the class with a regimented, Christian curriculum. A welcome albeit much different style than I had previously experienced. We covered a lot of the stuff I saw as a teen in Tang Soo Do. Punches, kicks, blocks, and kata.

The class consisted of ten people at the time. Two of whom were Master Winter's daughters, the rest church members, and one of whom, again, was my buddy, Andrew Baker.

I had a good time training there, appreciated the warm ups, the structured self-defense drills, and the sparring with Andrew. He lasted a year and a half, and I continued for the duration of my years at design school.

I learned a lot in class, and I attended a few social events at the church. I studied under Master Winter for four belt levels. In my final double stripe yellow belt test, I performed several kata and broke a board. I surprised myself.

The class helped me with confidence and discipline, helped me physically, strengthening me, postponing my CP-related atrophy. It also helped expand my creative process. I submitted a number of karate-oriented projects at school.

S PEAKING OF IMPROVED strength and creativity. It was early winter at the AI apartment when I had one of my worst seizures and required both qualities.

During my late night seizures, at the time, I felt as though I'd lost something, obsessively searched a premise for the loss, and aimlessly wandered.

Sometimes, I transported bed covers, clothes, mail, you name it, from room to room, moved lamps, unplugged lights; Other times, I went back to bed or sat on the couch, no rhyme or reason for my actions. Worse yet, I sometimes obsessed and didn't remember a thing.

At 12:30 AM, I came back to consciousness from one of my obsessive, wandering seizures, outside my apartment in short sleeve, boxers, and bare feet.

I looked under the front wheel of a car for my glasses as a heavy snow fell around me. I sifted through the dirt. Checked a light beam reflecting off the hubcap. But like most occasions, I finally realized my glasses were safe and sound indoors.

Wet and cold and at last lucid, I looked at the brick, apartment exterior with its narrow overhang, walked to my front door and tried to open it. But it was locked. My keys and cell phone were in my pants inside.

I put my knuckles to the door and rapped, to no avail. I waited a minute, closed my eyes, and then resorted to more force. I pounded with a heavy fist for several minutes. Still nothing.

Nobody outside, I huddled under the porch roof in the dark. The air was cold, and all I could do was shake my head and shiver. It was an incredibly lonely and helpless feeling. I knocked on the window panes, but nobody answered.

Hours passed, and my feet turned red, a little numb yet also hurting. I was sure I would soon experience Hypothermia.

I did pray; A sad, angry prayer. My chest surged. My teeth chattered. I paced. A thought did hit me around 3 AM. If I ran out back, I could throw a walnut or two at my housemates' second floor window. Perhaps I would wake them, and they'd let me in.

Fortunately, my aim was spot on. I had a throw that landed the objects right where I needed them. The nuts hit the glass with a thud. One time. Two times.

My housemates opened the window. "Seriously Josh? What is it?"

"I'm sorry guys. I've been out here all night. I'm freezing!"

"Geez dude."

"Can you please just let me in?"

They shook their heads in disgust. "Just a minute."

I thanked God as I walked inside and up the stairs to my bedroom. I thanked Him some more as I put on gym pants and socks and rubbed my feet until feeling returned.

ATER IN MY last semester, I rubbed my arm, where a needle piercing marked my vein. For the first time, I gave blood to the Salvation Army, inside one of those mobile medical vehicles parked outside the school. The Art Institute had a strong fund-raising base, and I decided to help.

Stepping out of the vehicle, however, I felt weak and dizzy. The phlebotomist was good. And yet I felt bad. Had I made a mistake, perhaps interfering with my medicine? I bought trail mix at the school store to quickly strengthen me. I had math class in a few minutes.

The classroom was small, the long tables pressed together in tight rows. Just enough space for white, plastic chairs and the students. Three to a table, coats and bags included.

Still sick, I made it through half the class. I escaped injury because of the confines, nevertheless I lost control and had a severe Grand Mal that paralyzed me for a good forty minutes. Nothing unusual yet; Just another day in the life.

When the Student Services staff tried to remove me from the room, however, I couldn't think or move. I was a dead weight. A few minutes later, after another try, I tripped and fell. No Golden Chariot around.

I didn't wear a belt that day, and as each woman tried to lift me again, arm in arm on either side of me, like a criminal muscled to his cage, I stumbled out, delirious from exhaustion yet concerned about my loose pants.

Heaving, I hooked a finger around my back, belt loop to maintain a semblance of dignity.

D ISCONTENT WITH MY final A.S. portfolio grade, a C, I decided I needed more practice, and pursued my second Bachelors. After all, I was so close to a better degree!

Around the same time I received an invite to look into a Doctoral program at Penn State Harrisburg. It was a five-year program. And I felt good about the opportunity. I was intrigued by God's timing, too. When I showed to the Open House, however, I was the only student of numerous existing teachers in need of more credentials, and it didn't seem to be the right direction just then.

Following more prayer, I convinced The Art Institute to financially cover me, went over my transcripts again with the program head, discovered additional classes to transfer, and prepared for another year of design training and refinement.

As an A.S. graduate, I made Deans List and earned a Scholars Honorarium plaque. I was pleased with my overall academic performance, yet I knew I could still grow.

To continue for my Bachelor of Science in Design was one of my best decisions. The Lord affirmed the decision by making the transition fluid. And, while tough, my last year was very rewarding.

I did an internship with Habitat for Humanity and Re-Source York, learning a lot about the nonprofit world; About designing despite the limited resources, and completing the creative process with hard work, sacrifice, and dedication.

I again participated in a school improvement session, similar to the graduate Climate Committee, called the Presidential Meeting. We highlighted effective processes, discussed specific concerns, and suggested special measures that could be taken to enhance the academic experience.

I later took a poetry class, which inspired me to write a few noteworthy rhymes. I then competed in a poetry competition hosted by the York County Poet-Laureate. I earned a third place ribbon the evening of the reading.

I also sat through many other design courses—typographic, vector, raster, and concept development—and finished by again taking portfolio prep and portfolio, which entailed repeated assembly attempts and presentation before peers and professors. By year's end, I justified my design in my sleep.

I got an A in the second portfolio class and the Bachelors Degree. I also created my current corporate identity, a digital portfolio, and an updated résumé.

PART FOUR

Freelance

2013-2019

35
FINEST PIECE

I N THE IMMEDIATE aftermath of school, I did stay in York. Again briefly at my parents' home. And what transpired next set into motion a series of events that I wouldn't fully grasp and appreciate until later in my career.

At the time, I didn't know how to feel about my job or living situation. I wanted my education to amount to independence, responsibility, and success, preferably in a timely manner. But I also knew I had to trust God's timing and synonymously remain productive. Which led me back to my pride and joy, fine art.

A Huntingdon Art League veteran by now, I knew each instructor annually introduced different techniques, some appealing, some not.

For instance, one year, it was flower painting. Another year, it was pastel landscapes. Another still, it was burnished colored pencil on riveted Mei Tientes water-color paper.

Though a foreign concept, the last yielded perhaps my finest piece. In the tight basement of a Huntingdon Catholic church (the Lion's Barn wasn't available this year), after watching a demonstration with my grandma, I shaped in a large cat. I started pressing in the color until I achieved a shiny gloss. Layer by layer for five straight days, I did this.

The burnished Bengal Tiger that emerged was as mysterious and surprising a project as any in my arsenal.

Pastel on suede was my specialty, but the colored pencil presented a more physically and emotionally demanding alternative that somehow released a new level of experimentation and creativity.

I still saw and created things in parts and layers, and I moved around the paper to get the job done. Developing the picture, however, I recognized new mark-making and color choice possibilities.

I grew as an artist that week. I realized certain ways to enhance and solidify my work. I embraced a new level of patience, which I've also seen since continues to evolve.

I had won all the art show ribbons except for the highly-coveted Best of Show. Every year, it escaped me. I had even accepted that my style was just too realistic.

That is, until I finally earned it with this drawing. And the expression on my grandma's face when we saw the competition results? Priceless.

S HOW AFTER SHOW, the Lord used that Tiger picture. "It has an especially warm feel," said my friend, Andrew. I agreed and also found it inviting. My grandma and I had spent an ample amount of time on the mat and frame, which made it pop. Whatever the case, it seemed to present more opportunity than any previous piece to date.

For two weeks, I showed it at the York Art Association. Another week, I showcased at The York County Fair, taking first place. I then had the chance to hang it at The Art Institute, and The Common Grounds at Living Word.

What was it about this piece that preceded so much blessing?

I N 2013, THE state advertised an art competition, to find and honor Pennsylvania talent and assemble twelve superior illustrations for their annual PADES calendar. I learned there were over three hundred applicants, and I decided to apply.

If you won, you acquired a small cash prize, a place in the calendar, and a free, three-day stay at The Hershey Lodge for the duration of the PADES conference, which included a night to publicly receive a plaque for the win.

How neat would it be to showcase a selection at the conference and in a calendar?

I inquired about the application process, submitted the Tiger as a digital image, and waited for the outcome.

A couple weeks passed before I learned the result. Competitions could be humbling experiences. I had accepted plenty of Honorable Mentions in my day. But I hoped to place, and place well, as I always wanted to achieve my goal.

The Tiger had been a winner, and I was proud of it. Of three hundred applicants, however, I didn't expect first place. And yet that is what I earned.

AFTER AN HOUR-LONG ride from York to Hershey, I walked into the Hershey Lodge. Andrew accompanied me, as I was allowed to invite a second person to enjoy the three-day stay, the conference, the food.

The lobby had a big stone hearth encircled by maroon leather seats; A perfect place to write later if I wanted. It also had a couple rafters overhead, adding a rugged touch.

I took in half of it, and then took in the other half. The ambiance reminded me of that which surrounded the cabin my grandparents and parents yearly leased for our family reunions. Granted, in contrast, the hotel offered plenty of space, which I always appreciated.

The vouchers I retrieved at the front desk covered all expenses. They gave Andrew and me full access to the on-site accommodations: Mini golf, the pool, the restaurants, a free breakfast the morning of the award ceremony. We took advantage of each activity and had a lot of fun before the big event.

Our second day, we even traveled to the Hershey Chocolate Factory. We were chosen to taste experimental candy bars and complete a subsequent poll. Andrew and I took home a few samples.

My grandparents and parents agreed to meet us on the third day, an hour prior to the ceremony. It was an exciting time.

I took pictures with my family and the PADES competition reps. I met different artists and answered questions. And, finally, I helped assemble a tall easel and put my Tiger on display.

The room was large and ornate. Crown molding and wainscoting added an eloquent accent. Curtains hung in various places along the perimeter. I had to hand it to the state; They picked a nice venue.

I was dressed up. Andrew was dressed up. We all were, really. And my entire family just seemed genuinely happy and proud. I was happy and proud, that's for sure.

The crowd wasn't thick. Rather, it was comprised of just enough. The clapping wasn't aura-inducing. Instead, it was light, steady, and enjoyable.

The PADES staff thanked the participating artists, announced the runners up and second place winners who walked up to acquire their honors, and then called me to the lectern to accept my first place win.

I got my calendar, my money, and my plaque. After a simple thank you and a few more pictures next to the Tiger, the crowd applauded some more. And I sat , feeling an awesome sense of accomplishment.

Accolades were great. But sharing accolades with the people I loved was far more rewarding.

36
ENTERTAINING IDEAS

NOW THAT I had finished my third degree, the Bachelor of Science (B.S.) in Graphic Design, and won a résumé-worthy award with the Tiger, I was back to identifying a profession. I worked with The AI York Career Services office and interviewed a number of times for jobs.

I spent a lot of time on the phone talking with independent job recruiters, as well, who forwarded potential job interviews with various firms if I took the necessary steps.

I eventually landed a freelance design job creating letterheads, logos, and signage for local nonprofit, Crispus Attucks. It was a successful job, albeit short-lived.

I created nice corporate identities, my strength, but for only about three months.

I also interviewed with and created a potential website for a company called Insolex, although that didn't go my way. They decided to hire a younger web designer.

Once finished, I had a lot of free time. So, I pulled out my previous writings, and entertained the idea of publishing.

My dad first paid me five dollars to write illustrated fiction. Around age ten, I transitioned to the short story. I tried my hand at it throughout high school, had to submit numerous short stories at Edinboro University, and in between counseling sessions and my thesis at Penn State University, I compiled a number of scenes for a novel. Here and there in Philly, I also created some additional scenes for a separate work.

Why not make good use of my time and attempt to make a dream a reality?

In 2012, self-publishing was coming into its own. I had briefly looked online, into Amazon's publishing subsidiary, CreateSpace, now known as Kindle Direct Publishing (KDP). In time, I'd explore Lulu and Nook Press, similar self-publishing outlets. Even so, I didn't jump right into it.

That same year, I Facebook friended a former CSY classmate finishing a CreateSpace-published suspense novel of her own. She took some time out of her day to answer my questions and explain what she knew.

I subsequently revisited CreateSpace, taught myself how to professionally prepare my work for the company, and moved ahead with the process. The best part of it was that it required all the skills I naturally possessed, and that I refined at school on three separate occasions.

In 2013, I published my first novella, *Grand Mal*, and my first novel, *Memory Lapse*. A kind, English professor I knew from AI York, Mr. George Rutledge, edited both manuscripts, and I designed the covers.

I put myself on a two-book-a-year artificial deadline for the next five years. And yet I remained focused on the day-to-day process required to complete a singular manuscript.

I submitted everything, and soon I was selling on Amazon, Apple, Smashwords, and numerous other distribution sites.

37
IN NO TIME

WITHIN A FEW weeks, I moved from my parents basement into a small box of a house on a side road across from Suburban Bowlerama. There were three of us, all single, independent men living there, each so different from one another; I rented the back bedroom, painted a dark navy blue, for six months.

During that six months, I faced a lot of uncertainty. Even so, I stuck to my regiment. When in doubt, I believed, push ahead in faith. I still had heavy auras, sporadic Grand Mals, but I daily walked along the narrow berm to Subway and wrote in my usual spot, the far recliner before the circular table.

The Lord provided occasional design projects, and when I wasn't penning a story, I was designing a book cover, editing, illustrating, or offering my general two-cents on various matters of art and publishing.

I still wasn't working in an official capacity, and yet I had been approached about prospective employment as a student, which gave me hope and caused me to go back to that day. I honestly believe no encounter happens without a reason, and that one on Portfolio Day was no different.

"YOU'LL BE EMPLOYED in no time," said the tall redhead, Ken Kinard of Accent Interactive, handing me a card emblazoned with its geometric, purple logo. "I guarantee it."

I stood behind a long white table, my leather portfolio open, my business cards at the front, my Tiger on display and my 3-D 'Ape Juice' juice box creation angled just so. I collected the card, stuffed it in my pocket, and said, "Thank you! I'll be in touch."

It was perhaps the most promising statement I heard from all the people that walked through the Strand Capital Theatre (currently The Appell Center for the Performing Arts) and examined my presentation on Portfolio Day.

It was a great day; A busy day. My peers and I spent hours preparing for the grand finale. All my family and friends showed throughout the day to enjoy and support my fine art, design work, and memorized portfolio piece explanations.

I prayed ahead of time that the Lord would protect me, and allow me a disruption-free day, as in a Grand Mal-free day. I didn't have any big spells, but I still performed despite plenty of stimulation and an undercurrent of aura in my eyes and stomach.

A selfish request? Perhaps.

In any event, the possibility of immediate employment assured me when the show was over and in the days to come.

I did wonder, *A job with him? Or just a job, in general?*

So, I called the number on the card, found out Ken was an eccentric life coach and web designer heavily focused on creativity.

I had a meeting with him at a Pancra in the fall of 2013. I shared my life story, my job goals, and he invited me to one of his upcoming six-week classes that addressed creativity and web-development, specifically in WordPress.

MY DAD WAS kind enough to transport me back and forth to Hunt Valley, where the classes took place. I sometimes caught a return ride with one of the staff members, Chris, who also attended the Art Institute when I did.

Accent Interactive was attached to Ken's home. A bright work/classroom, it was full of computer terminals and suited the staff. An overhead projector was mounted on the front wall. It also served as an adequate meeting place for other creative activities.

Ken's WordPress seminar primarily unfolded there, covering all the details. Ken taught us some web coding, HTML and CSS, how to upload media, to create pages, posts, and generally to navigate the interface. He disclosed ways to improve SEO.

I worked on a number of possible logos for an Accent Interactive client; Generated numerous potential corporate identity directions, anyway. Ken liked some; The feedback seemed positive.

Beyond the work/classroom, I participated in an Accent Interactive activity in York that was intended to stir the imagination and jog the creative juices. With a pre-assigned partner, I designed a picture out of fruit randomly purchased from the Central Market.

I hoped for a future job while participating but didn't know where it all was leading.

At the end of the six weeks, I didn't acquire a job with the company. I did, however, learn how to develop websites.

I would gladly persist, turn the skill set into money, offering the service to personal clients in the years that followed.

38
RETURN TO THE DOJO

JOINED A league at the Suburban Bowlerama a week after the web design course concluded. An ardent fan, I completed the first with two pros who improved my game. I then updated my bowling apparel, and I earned a runner up trophy with a second assigned teammate.

After leaving the box house rental and moving a mile away into York Apartments, I joined a third tournament with my friend, Dan McDermott. We fared well against superior bowlers and earned a first-place trophy in our first competition as teammates.

Flashing lights and constant crashing within, I had auras nearly every time I entered the alley. Second to a crowded auditorium, it was the most stimulating place a person with uncontrolled epilepsy could walk into.

I had experienced a couple traumatic Grand Mals prior to and during the tournament. Even so, I tried to play every night.

One seizure, in particular, was so upsetting, the Lord allowed me to disconnect. A bold claim, I know. But I remember floating above the event, in a warm, consolidated space, watching it all unfold.

After I took a fall under a table, I observed a lady rush over, whip back a chair, lift my head from the sparkly carpet, and place it in her lap.

My cries and labored breathing led to more confusion, to scared people grasping for control.

Without a word, one frightened girl stepped away, phoned 911, and disappeared into the crowd.

Moments later, like Sumo wrestlers, two mammoth men started bumping chests, arguing over my dead body about what should happen.

"Just walk away, man. I don't want trouble. Give the guy space." Bump.

"I'm the EMT, bud. Just doing my job. Get out of the way!" Bump.

"Not going anywhere! I'm in charge of the alley, tonight. Managing the situation!" Bump.

A girlfriend or sister added her two-cents, preceding a pause, and then ending the feud.

When the manager conceded, I returned from afar, once again a part of the actual incident. I looked up, and tried to move, to get up and out of there.

The events that transpired gave me enough material to pen my next novel, *Trigger*.

I experienced God's mercy that night. And yet the ordeal impacted me enough that I reconsidered my future participation.

"WHAT WOULD YOU think about pursuing something more physically demanding?" I said to Dan our last night at the alley. "I was thinking about getting back into karate. Looking for a reasonably-priced class."

A thin, quiet, agreeable guy who had driven me to The York Alliance Church, to growth group meetings, various social activities, and the bowling alley, Dan accepted the possibility without objection.

To cover my bases, I said, "Just say no if you don't want to."

"No. I mean, yeah. I'm willing to try it out."

I thought about returning to Mike's program at the church, as I enjoyed it. But I also looked at all my options, to see if there was anything closer. I came across York Shotokan Mixed Martial Arts, a nonprofit club.

"I talked to the Sensei today," I said. "Would you be open to taking a ride out there, to watch and meet with him?"

ANOTHER SMOOTH TRANSITION for Dan and me affirmed my return to the dojo. I believed the direction was a wise one and a part of the ultimate Plan.

I'll admit, though, that I did make our first night an interesting one. I mistakenly suggested we wear our gis to the dojo, thereby earning our first public scolding.

We had a good, introductory interview too. After I gave Sensei Abel the run down regarding my personal information and history in and beyond the study, Dan offered the same, and Sensei Abel directed us to take the next steps.

He looked back at me and reiterated, "I refuse to treat you any differently."

And I nodded. "Fair enough."

The dojo was bright and spacious. Half wooden floors. Half floor mats. A thick white curtain divider. Floor-to-ceiling mirrors reflected our images in improper attire, on all four sides, and the Shotokan Tiger glared at us, as if our actions offended him in some way.

Dan and I apologized and rushed to the locker room.

In the first week, while doing sit ups, I pushed myself and after years of neck pulls, I heard and felt the scar tissue surrounding my Vagus nerve rip free, a bizarre sense of freedom and ache coursing through me.

I healed quickly and we attended twice a week for about two years. It quickly proved to be more of a mental challenge than a physical one, although it was taxing on my body, too. And we succeeded in being diligent and in climbing the ranks.

Dan was a good listener. After a tough class, he let me unload about my frustrations. And he shared his opinions with me.

I did take longer to fight with control. My CP, general imbalance, and sensory deficit were difficult to work around. And my experience in dojos past involved heavy contact.

Dan was my partner when trying to figure things out; The recipient of my struggle. But my path had always been different, no matter who or how someone journeyed with me.

I did eventually make a conscious decision to brawl with restraint. I had to consciously decide to adjust a number of things, as I didn't immediately notice a lot. I finally saw that at the dojo, when tired, my body's right side responded with less precision. The lightbulb moment evaded me, however, until after Dan informed me of his plan to leave.

Every week I was pushed beyond my limits. Through unceasing repetition. Through intense runs and somersaults that elicited auras. Exercises that required deeper breathing. Sparring that demanded intense focus. Even so, I resolved to hold firm.

39
MAKE A WAY

EARLY IN MY stay at York Apartments—this time on Bristol Drive, two roads up from Brentwood Drive—I lived alone. I was thrilled to complete the Wordpress class, to perform well in a league and an eventual dojo, and move out of the box house, into my own pad.

However, I still didn't really know what my future entailed, or for how long this place would be my home. I had signed onto a year lease, but I was hesitant to decorate it or call it my own. Even with a number of scheduled design projects, I realized it would be tight and that the

Lord would have to make a way. As He promised he would.

My unit, 303 F, was built in the sixties, so it was old and ready for total renewal. The walls were thin, the floors creaky, the doors scarred, and yet it was on the main floor, and I had a nice porch. The layout was open, airy, and ideal. I could comfortably walk from room to room without concern for my safety.

Numerous things transpired while living here my first year, but perhaps the three most distinct pursuits I attempted to set into motion and consistently sought were my freelance career, non-medicinal medical treatments, and spiritual/emotional healing.

A FEW MONTHS into my new rental, it just so happened that I met Knittel and Angela Ansa—a motivated, Christian entrepreneurial couple, not yet married but getting there.

It was a God thing, for I needed employment and they needed a starter website and corporate identity for their pending Prosthetics and Orthotics venture, Aspire Prosthetics, which now has expanded to multiple locations due to their quality service.

Knittel, a smart, happy, and genuine guy, initially examined my right foot when I was dealing with strong aura and my Cerebral Palsy was causing me severe ankle and sole pain, nearly debilitating me. In doing so, he pinpointed the problem and assured me that he could resolve the matter. We then struck up a conversation in his office about my own profession.

"So Josh, you are an artist."

I showed him a few pieces on my phone. "Yes I am, actually. But I also am a designer. Web design, graphic design, logos, you name it."

"Web design and logos, huh," said Knittel. "Do you have a card?"

"I do."

Knittel recognized my address and told me he also lived at York Apartments.

Before I knew it, Knittel and Angela stopped by my place for a consultation, and together we discussed concept and design and demographic, assembled a website, after which we agreed on a logo for the company. I learned a lot through our blunt exchanges.

The statement, "One's connection improves selection", proved true for me in the next couple months. I completed the design jobs, got paid, but, following the transition from Ability to Aspire Prosthetics, it didn't stop there. Knittel continued to be a friend and treat my right foot.

He again came over to my place, wrapped my foot in plaster of paris and, as I sat there on the couch, he shaped an insert for my shoe that compensated for the atrophy. It alleviated my discomfort.

Before moving on with their lives, they each read my books, *Grand Mal* and *Seizure*, and were kind enough to write me a set of positive reviews.

God not only financially made a way in the beginning, He also introduced me to two people whom I could personally benefit, and who, in return, could bless me spiritually, professionally and physically.

40
ON A ROLL

SEEKING INCOME FOR my second room, I signed a
lease with a wiry, general laborer named Aaron. He
unloaded trucks for a company he'd unhappily been
with forever, but he made a good living, enjoyed cooking
a mean steak, marinated in a signature sauce and olive
oil, and valued a clean house like me. For the most part,
we got along.

Aaron was a protective brother to me. He was frightened by my seizures, but if he could do anything to help
make our lives easier he did attempt to do so.

I did have to tip-toe around Aaron, for he excessively
drank alcohol. From the time he arrived home to the time

he retreated to his bedroom, he scowled and tossed his things. After a few refills, he calmed and slept, his CPAP machine vibrating in the background.

Even so, for three years we co-existed, ate together, and talked politics, sports, disability, relationships, and Christianity, in depth. I tried to be an objective, non-judgmental sounding board for him.

We lived very different lives, and yet we each grew to appreciate one another.

ON A ROLL, I one day left the apartment with Aaron and sought a fix for the glasses that broke on me every time I seized and fell against my face. Little did I know what that quest would introduce.

I was thirty-six when I learned of the condition category, Photosensitive Epilepsy. But considering my sensitivity to light, I was immediately convinced that I had it.

I was in my eye doctor's office, just finishing an overview of the scenario that brought me, when one of the assistants printed out and handed me an article on a young girl who shared similar light triggers to me.

I took the article, thanked her, and sat in the empty reception area, perhaps fifteen feet away from the glistening, floor-to-ceiling racks of glasses, separated every few feet by full body mirrors.

The article went on to share how a specific blue-hued lens, Zeiss Z1 F133 (cobalt), protected the girl from certain wavelengths when watching TV and playing video games.

Why has my neurologist never told me of this? I wondered. *It seems so obvious.*

On second thought, it was a possible cure that neither entailed medicine, nor required surgery. And it was relatively inexpensive, all things considered.

"I believe this is what I have," I said, diagnosing myself on the spot. "Photosensitive Epilepsy, I mean. Is there any way you could look into this, and if so could I pursue a blue lens?"

Of late, the auras had been strong, I had morphed between worlds and fallen more than usual. The scars accumulated at the corners of my eyes and along my hairline, confirming this. So, I ordered some blue lens sunglasses while I waited for the appointment, to experiment.

I wore them when I ventured out, in the house, and to bed. There was no questioning it stopped some of the light-induced auras.

From my pant pocket, I pulled a folded pair that I brought as a reference. "I got these off of Amazon. They're cheap. But they darken everything, and I've seen a decrease in aura."

JAMES, MY EYE specialist at *Designer Family Eyecare*, came out to help the assistant. A lanky, dark-haired guy, he was especially kind and quickly took an interest in my request; He went above and beyond to help me acquire the lenses.

"You do realize the coating on the sunglasses is different than what you want on a poly-carbonate lens, right?"

"I don't know much beyond the article," I said, waving the paper back and forth. "The brand Zeiss. I'm trusting you to order the right stuff."

"Well, there is a difference."

"Let's go with your recommendation," I said.

"You want the colored poly-carbonates then."

It took us a couple tries, as we didn't technically pursue Zeiss, the brand, but rather a cobalt likeness. A few times the blue hue turned out too dark and too light. He also had to experiment in-house, which initially took longer and tied his hands. But he finally landed the happy medium that allowed me to see and generally test the theory.

In the first couple days of testing them, I was intrigued. I noticed my whole half world was a little darker. The light didn't seem to bother me to the extent that it once did.

At the same time, I still was sensitive to competing light wavelengths. I still seized and broke glasses if I watched certain shows or movies while on my computer or walked into restaurants like Jersey Mike's. So, similar to the VNS devices, they offered a degree of psychological comfort, but in the end they didn't stop the auras or Grand Mals.

I continue to wear the blue-lens glasses today, as they are availed to me. James is now a friend and stops by my apartment with upgrades as needed. I used this experience to chronicle my fifth book, *Status*. It was one more treatment possibility. But I can't say with any degree of certainty that the color has done for me what it did for the girl in the article.

Perhaps one day!

41
SUDDEN

U PON AARON'S DEPARTURE, I signed a lease with a Saudi Arabian, PSU-York transfer student named Ahmad. He majored in Engineering, as his country considered it valuable and many from that region who opt out of the oil industry and instead choose college go into the field.

We got along, he handled my seizures well, I was able to help him with English homework, and we even had a couple conversations about God and my Christian faith. I made sure to keep the dialogue casual, as I felt the Lord could take my commentary as far as He willed.

Several nights, over shared pizzas, I learned a lot about Saudi culture, about Ahmad's opinions of it. He, in turn, heard a lot about American culture, about my beliefs, how I had arrived at my viewpoints.

My housemate did start talking in a different language late into the night with other anonymous Internationals via his computer. It made me curious, more alert. And yet rent was covered every month, and the utilities were equally split.

I still hadn't decorated my place, and my published books were starting to accumulate on my side table. Ahmad's school semester passed quickly.

And then, suddenly, six months in, Ahmad vanished, never again to be seen.

A FEW WEEKS prior to Ahmad's disappearance, he helped with a seizure I had on the couch in my living room. In my delirium, I searched for money in the couch seams that wasn't there, but he was nice about it.

On the same couch the night Ahmad disappeared, after realizing he was gone, I made one last effort to reach out to him. Cell phone in my lap, I typed, "Where are you, Ahmad? Are you okay?"

"I'm lost in the deep woods of Washington D.C. Haha."

I curled up under a blanket and raised my eyebrows. *What in the world?*

It took a few days to get over Ahmad's immediate absence, and I did wonder whether he had run off and involved himself in some form of foreign deviance, but—as was my normal tendency—I decided to pick myself up and get moving.

I had sought and found a solution for the pain in my feet and the stimuli in my eyes. Now I wanted to address some accumulated body pain. And I again had some alone time to do so.

I N THE QUIET, I considered my past injuries and subsequent coping strategy. I didn't do anything unique; I simply addressed seizure-related injury either through prayer, painkiller and tolerance, or, in the severe cases, through more prayer, chiropractic care and long-term physical therapy.

In most cases, during a seizure I turned to the right and twisted all the way back before the fall, straining neck and shoulder, and pulling back muscles. These strains and pulls subsequently caused awful head pain until treated.

True, I had a sensory deficit in my right side. And yet, I also had what I would call abrupt phantom pains in spurts. I have a high pain tolerance; Even so, I took some spills that were just agonizing.

In 2014, after a morning meeting I tipped back in a chair at Starbucks while talking on the phone. Subconsciously, I was discouraged about the earlier consult. Mid-conversation, my speech left me, and I dropped the phone.

Against my will, I twisted ninety degrees, as if someone latched onto my chin, yanked from behind, attempting a head snap. The person sitting nearby failed to catch me, and as a result my skull connected and bounced like a basketball on a court.

It was the most direct impact I'd ever taken, which then preceded months of tightness and dull yet exhausting head pain. I was diagnosed with a concussion.

I did take a similar fall in 2012 while at the Art Institute. For lunch, I walked to Rutters, just opposite of the school and Springetsberry Township Park.

When waiting in a long line to purchase a hotdog and tea, the auras in my eyes elevated into a Generalized seizure. Without warning, I fell straight back. My food and drink rolled, my computer bag flew, and I anticipated a hard hit.

In this instance, however, I wore a golf cap, and subsequently connected with a fabric buffer. It wasn't much protection, although it offered more than what I had in Starbucks.

In December of the same year, I went on to describe the Starbucks event and personal pain management efforts in depth in my third, self-published book, *Seizure*.

A S A RESULT of the injuries and the rising cost of chiropractic care, in 2014 I went in search of an alternate treatment. I was pleasantly surprised when I learned Wellspan Rehabilitation was located just feet from my apartment.

Within a week I was walking to the office at Queensgate Plaza and signing in for my first evaluation.

I began the first week of several years to come worth of physical therapy. I had good rapport with all my therapists, and again I had substantive conversation, not only addressing the mundane, but also life struggles, and the spiritual. To an extent, in some instances, I was again acting as a counselor, even as I too received wise counsel.

I heard a teacher once speak to the spiritual significance of a person's geographical location. I didn't consider my proximity to Wellspan Rehab until I was on my fourth treatment plan to remedy repeat seizure injuries. But I eventually did think there was something to that.

Every other day, I worked with my physical therapists to ward off pain and atrophy. We spent time on my right ankle, my right foot, my right scapula, my right shoulder, my right neck and head.

Some days they tugged at the muscle fascia, while other days they loosened tight nerves. Some days they applied ultrasound gel and massaged me. And other days they instructed me as I worked on balance and general strengthening.

Because insurance companies had to see clear progression, that was a significant goal. If through my story and efforts I could encourage my therapists to persist, that was also a personal goal of mine.

42
SIMILARITIES

LATER I LEASED a room to AJ, a Christian young man with autism. At the time of the agreement, I didn't know of his condition. He was a genuinely nice guy in his early twenties, looking to be independent. And he also was especially sensitive about my seizures, as he had a younger brother with special needs.

I left the house and kept busy during the day, returned at night in hopes of relaxing. He said he worked, he talked of construction, although I had no way of knowing until rent was due.

It was alright, at first. I didn't mind what AJ did, as long as he was law-abiding, clean, respectful, and civil. We spent a few nights discussing Christianity and certain theological positions that troubled him.

Weeks went by, though, and I started noticing behaviors I saw from the young adults I coached at Lifelink PSU and CareerLink and in housemates at the Art Institute: Major neglect of basic life responsibilities (e.g. changing dress, garbage removal, going to work, and, most concerning, rent). He also loudly played video games for days in the dark, excited about online connections, even as he was afraid to connect with people in-person.

My apartment grew increasingly messy, smelly, and loud. I heard all manner of noises come out of his bedroom.

A local church friend and leader aware of my physical conditions and of AJ's history expressed concern about his spiritual state and about the living arrangement. He recommended ending it.

I was unsure of the suggestion, confused at what to do; Prayed a lot about it. The thought of hosting evil in my home, though, ultimately scared me.

I was able to sit and talk with AJ, albeit a soft, counselor/client conversation, about my observations and concerns.

"AJ. I sure didn't anticipate this," I said. "I needed a housemate. But I've been advised to have you leave."

"So you just do what others tell you to do?"

"I consider the advise of wise people."

"But we've done well here."

"I'm actually not thrilled with the mess the apartment has turned into."

"And you won't tell me who has advised you?"

"I can't do that."

And though my housemate was upset, we had a civil discussion about his spiritual state, about possible perceptions of his history, and we agreed to part ways.

The ordeal, unsettling though it was, allowed me to clarify to my concerned friend that AJ, in fact, had a disability. While online gaming had turned sinister in recent years, his behavior wasn't due to addiction or possession. In my opinion, they aligned with typical autistic tendencies.

I hoped this clarification would help AJ as he moved forward.

MEANWHILE, THE NATIONAL Seizure Disorder Foundation (NSDF), an online epilepsy support network, reached out to me to push my novels in the Grand Mal Series, to tell my story and affirm to its viewers what persons with epilepsy are capable of.

My immediate friends and family liked the idea of having me speak in public. My dad, in particular, often pushed the idea. As a writer who mostly worked in the background, I was less inclined. But this was an overt request, and, frankly, a great marketing opportunity. I complied.

After telling my story to a number of men and women living with epilepsy, answering multiple questions, the organization asked me to contribute in the area of art and web design. I cleaned a few program character icons and put together some banners.

I worked tirelessly to assist the organization. Introduced new ideas. Went to meetings. My book and art sales increased for a period as my network with the epilepsy community blossomed.

It kept me occupied as my second room was again vacated, as I interviewed possible candidates, and the search for a new roommate continued.

WITH EACH NEW roommate, it seemed amid the living complexities that the Lord afforded me a new area of physical healing. In the fall of 2016, after working with NSDF, and then four months of online dating and a failed relationship attempt, He protected me from a disaster and went a step further, introducing a means of emotional healing.

I didn't expect to return to school again; I'd done it for so long! And yet when I saw the ad for The Unveiling Prophetic School one Sunday at church, I felt compelled to sign up. I was up for an academic and spiritual challenge too.

I had an opportunity to change that false self definition and perception of God that I developed as a teen and previously associated with the Christian schools in which I grew up, to rid of the seizure-related guilt and fear, the self-blaming, and angry God view. So I took full advantage.

It was interesting to observe how satan attempted to interfere. On the dot, every Saturday night at 12 PM, I went into a Grand Mal. As if exhausting me physically

and psychologically would force me to skip and keep
me from the Sunday night transformation.

Aware of this, though, I asked the Lord for supernatural power and protection and fought through it every
week. I went into The Praise Community auditorium,
steeped in aura, my white notebook and homework
before me at one of the long white tables, and situated
myself next to my friend, Kim Trostle.

The class really did present a safe space to discuss
revelations, approach God and experience His presence.

I was thrilled to get to a place of self forgiveness
and to see God my Father as One who isn't out to
punish me but to love me. Even though escaping injury
was still a priority, and my sight deficit still induced
claustrophobia, I was able to move away from the idea
of self preservation and start looking for new ways to
share love with others.

I was encouraged to grow in my relationship
with God.

43
PRAYERS

MOST RECENTLY, IN 2017, I leased a room to a nice African American man named Lamont. Tired and wielding a visible limp, he expressed that his mother just died, that he was living in a hotel, and that he needed an immediate place to stay.

He also informed me he'd had a stroke, that he had high blood pressure, severe pain and anxiety. The number of conditions gave me pause, and yet, having conditions of my own, I felt it was only right to give him the benefit of the doubt. My seizures didn't alarm him either.

He knew I was a believer. I still took The Unveiling prophecy class when he was living here. And after discussing what I learned, he appeared to make an effort to get involved with a different local church.

Even so, he obsessed about acquiring money, especially for rent and utilities; This, after he assured me he could fulfill his financial responsibilities, no problem. He spent a lot of time on the phone trying to get friends to cover him. Why so much worry?

The worry continued, though, and grew exponentially. It started branching out into everything.

I would ask, "How are you doing this morning?" or "So what's your plan for the day?"

"What's it to you? Why do you care what I'm doing today?"

"Just trying to be nice is all."

"Stop looking at me like that!"

Is he experiencing paranoia? I wondered. *Having hallucinations?*

Weeks passed, the exchanges between us still hostile. I was at a loss, but in time I would receive an answer to my question.

He was found downtown under the influence of alcohol and drugs and was charged. That same night, he arrived at my home an even wilder person. He went back to his room, and he intensely talked on the phone with his pastor. He whimpered, wailed, shouted, exploded for six hours.

Angry at and frightened by the endless, erratic behavior, at 1 AM I knocked on the door. He opened it, and I said, "Lamont. It's late. What's going on?"

Like a little boy, he covered his face, said, "Please no. Don't hurt me! Get away!"

"It's me, Lamont. Your housemate, Josh," I said. "Why would I hurt you?" I encouraged him to sit on our couch in the living room. I told him he wasn't himself, and I asked if he had consumed something. He denied it. "I think we need to pray."

With Lamont's pastor on the phone, I lay a hand on him and prayed. He calmed for an hour.

S O GOD HAD given me physical, emotional, and spiritual healing, but—as is usually the case—He wasn't through. After Lamont left, He revealed Himself through dietary healing.

Shortly after my latest appointment with James, I ate at *Tropical Smoothie Paradise*, situated at the rear of a strip mall just across the way from *Designer Family Eyecare*. I thought if I had a protein drink I'd be set. Rap music blaring in the background, though, I didn't stop to consider all the sugar. How could I overlook that?

The energy and lights in that place kept me on guard. And how about the loud, industrial air ducts? I looked at the ground, avoiding stimuli, before eventually inquiring about the order.

The employees took their time, but were finally able to pull themselves away from the latest catering order and create my drink and wrap.

I took it, sat at the nearest, neon metal stool and table, and gulped that big cup of Peanut Butter Paradise. Ate my peanut butter and banana honey wrap too.

Not a great idea. But the result taught me what to consume and what to avoid.

I learned that if I didn't eat a protein by 10 AM I seized by 2 PM. If not a fat by 12 AM I seized by 7 AM. It was hard, and I was weary of it. And so, I left the electric establishment, and started revising my intake.

I couldn't go so far as to declare my epilepsy controlled, although after that evening I went from experiencing three Grand Mals every two weeks to four every five weeks.

I went from many sleepless nights interrupted by multiple sugar-induced seizures to a few every month and a week. Granted, that didn't address the light-induced seizures, although it protected me longer in places that contained bright triggers.

With an increase in protein-rich and fatty foods, the auras decreased considerably. I was able to view the world more normally for longer periods of time.

After years of medicinal experimentation, my blood test levels always came back low. Even though I was toxic, the doctors wanted to increase my pill number.

I realized it wasn't about taking too few pills. In fact, the pills weren't staying inside me long enough to cover me. Theoretically, slowing its consumption would improve the chances of it working.

I stayed away from bread. The items I chose were eggs and cheese and nuts, food kinds that didn't speed up metabolism, but rather offered padding for my pills and lasted longer in my system.

It was a balancing act, and it was easy to lose track of the day's meals. I did every few weeks. But I now had more of an answer than I ever previously had.

Friends did counsel me to keep a food journal. A suggestion I knew had merit, and that I intended to do, but that I never officially got around to.

I did, however, now have a healthy lifestyle to aspire to and one to sustain.

OVER THE NEXT few weeks, several seemingly random bouts of weakness from which I struggled to physically and mentally rebound caused me to further assess my consumption habits.

The first things that crossed my mind were the several instances I fought mouth sores. Cheek twitches. Drowsiness. They made me think about deficiency.

Was it possible I was lacking in vitamins and nutrients? And if so, which were we talking about? A select few that, in its absence, made me seize?

I watched a video on potassium and electrolyte deficiency, which spoke about my symptoms and prompted me to walk into GNC one Sunday afternoon.

"Do you happen to carry electrolyte powder," I said. "I believe I'm not getting enough."

The short cashier smiled and walked around the counter, eager to help.

"What do you mean 'not enough'?"

"I stay away from fruit," I said. "It makes me tired."

"And veggies?"

"Well, I have epilepsy, you see. And I also study the Martial Arts," I said. "I recently tried cutting sugar. It seems to help decrease the attacks, but when I grow too exhausted at the dojo, I also have seizures."

"So you think this powder will give you what you're not getting from fruit and veggies?"

"I'm hardly a food expert," I said "But it's worth a shot."

"We have an unflavored brand," said the rep, pointing at the second shelf. "But that's all."

"I'll take it," I said. "Thank you."

44
RECOVERY

AGAIN RETURNED to single living, to recover. I had lived through a lot. Complicated, scary circumstances, even as I worked, seized and battled.

After I prayed for Lamont, he slept. But, ultimately, he resumed where he left off. He refused to talk to me, to look at me. He squatted, and I had to wait weeks to return to normalcy.

He actually left the night of the 2017 Super Bowl, after a final ultimatum. I'd stayed a month in my parents' guest bedroom to avoid the situation. Lamont took my place from me. And I'd never been so happy to enter my own apartment.

In my case, something as simple as an open, furnished apartment bedroom not only led to total reliance on God, but also to uncanny opportunities to directly and indirectly influence those He put in my path, in ways even I, an artist and author, could neither have imagined nor created.

As I cleaned my apartment that night—and Lamont left quite a mess—I did wonder, *Does it get any wilder than that? Will there be more?*

MONTHS PASSED, AND for the first time I experienced the world even more clearly than I had in my mid-thirties. Like your everyday Joe, I figured. I still took Keppra XR and Depakote ER. But I felt balanced. I just ate healthily. I lost a lot of weight and physically felt good.

Perhaps I had to be alone during this period, to hear God, to identify the physical, emotional, and spiritual facets. The Lord works in mysterious ways, after all.

Whatever the case, I was grateful. I had stopped morphing into other worlds, stopped merging with different planes, walls, and floors, stopped going out anticipating an interruption of one kind or another.

I could also stare at my computer, TV, and movie screen without feeling off-kilter, without light stealing my freedom, without a magnetic pull sucking me into an alternate reality, as I always imagined my friends and family checked email and watched films.

It was hard to fathom. For thirty-eight years, I lived on this earth consumed by an inescapable dimension, an aura that made me feel so vulnerable and prone to danger.

I had the early, sin-related concerns. Fear about doing something wrong, something to deserve my conditions. And I was able to defeat those lies.

Now I could walk here and there, a part of the regular environment, a normal part of society, no interference to speak of. I could just soak it up.

Granted, I seized every six or seven weeks, but that was a substantial drop. So substantial, I risked the thought of a life without epilepsy.

At the very least, I could start talking about being controlled. Even though the neurologists always said I was the two percent that wouldn't respond to treatment.

More cognizant of triggers, I typically could attribute the seizures to sugar or caffeine consumption. Too little and too much. I did my best to avoid them, to stay home when I ate some, to eat in accordance with my activities, and continued to pray for total healing.

45
A GOOD DAY

A PRISM OF color, the sun shone on me through the window one fine afternoon in 2013, as if the Lord was affirming His presence and satisfaction with my plan for the day.

Its warmth inched up my forearm, settled in, and enveloped me as I sat at a round table and typed before a laptop.

"Today is the day," I said. "A good day to set JAHbookdesign into motion."

If again asked what I thought I might do following graduate and design schools, I would repeat "Whatever the Lord wills" and "Something in design, I imagine." And a little older and wiser, I'd also add, "But I wouldn't be surprised if I do something else entirely."

I likely wouldn't say, "Oh, I will work for myself" or "I will start my own self-publishing company." And yet, God saw far more than I did and led me in that direction.

At first, as corporate identities are supposed to do, the brand brought awareness. It professionally marketed my story and products and repeatedly exposed my network to my pursued projects. And I did see some interest.

Over time, however, He revealed that I should neither be the sole beneficiary of the interest, nor of all my training and experience. Instead, I should offer it as a service, and others should reap rewards.

Still in the warmth, I took a deep breath and soaked it up. It was bright in my eyes, but it felt right. A second later, the sun shifted away from my face, I confidently leaned forward, and I said, "Ok. Let's do this."

My personal website before me, I started establishing my web presence, redirecting web address nameservers, introducing my company story, my contact page, my products, and my service options.

I took my aforementioned brand, developed in school and applied to all my personal novel and eBook releases, updated my biographical information, and started pushing it on all design, social media, and publishing outlets.

I invited every aspiring author in my network to consider an alternate publishing method. An alternate provider of writing, editing, illustration, and advertising.

SEASONS MELTED INTO one another, but in each the Lord showed a sign at the window. A rainbow in the spring. Colored leaves in the autumn. Crystalline flakes in the winter.

JAHbookdesign didn't pull in a whole host of clients all at once. In The Lord's timing, my brand caught the attention of select artists, authors, and poets who reached out to me.

Morning, noon, and night, I always returned to the same restaurant table pushed tight against the glass, flipped open my laptop, and I gladly read notes from interested parties.

I won't name all my customers, as I've had quite a number over the years. And I won't get into the little things I've done behind the scenes. I hold the memories of my efforts close.

In my seat, I leaned over, extended, and pulled an index finger through the dust on the windowsill.

I had a few significant design jobs that afforded me the opportunity to indirectly share the Salvation message, however, and these are the jobs I'd like to speak to.

My friend and longest customer, Kyle Walker, approached me in 2012 to do a portrait of his grandma. Upon successful completion, I illustrated a cover for his latest book release, *Rainbows Hidden Treasures*, although it would not be used for the final product.

Nearly every year for the next six years Kyle and I worked on a new cover and refined manuscript to publish for his fan base and the unsaved. It was a collaborative effort that resulted in Kyle's comprehensive poetry catalogue.

After developing a logo for local companies Aspire Prosthetics and The Bank Pros, I collaborated with a client, Mandy Trostle, to refine and illustrate her children's book, *Abel the Alligator*. The Lord used that book to bless many adults and children around the world.

In 2018, after over a decade and a half, I again crossed paths with my childhood friend, flight attendant, author and poet, Marissa. She also had a story to tell and a vast poetry collection, and we worked together to prepare her covers and manuscripts for publication.

I could go on and on.

My epilepsy, CP, and sight were a constant fight. But I pushed through. And in my sixth year of self-employment now, The Lord continues to provide. I've never gone without work. Thirty-six self-published books. Six company websites. Six finalized corporate identities.

Outside, the sun settled in the distance. Its light reached for me one final time.

It will be exciting to see what comes next.

EPILOGUE
I SEE

I N LOOKING BACK at my life, I see why the Lord prompted me to tell my story. I see how much I did survive and accomplish through Christ, how in Him I can do all things. The deceiving cloud floated in at some point, but the Lord exposed it, and it has now moved on.

I am confident in the fact that I have seen the lies, and that with God I can identify any future clouds that roll in, rising above them before they again infiltrate.

If you desire the same confidence, I suggest you put your trust in The Only One who can give it to you, The Only One who can save you and help you defeat your clouds. The Only One who *wants* to assist you. It is possible!

Before my trusty easel I continue to plug away. To anticipate. In the way exclusive to me, I proceed with a new portrait. Left line, right line; Left part, right part; Left color, right color.

I believe that the Lord will continue to reveal to me new levels of experimentation and creativity, not to mention new revelations for personal growth, which will ultimately impact those around me.

I'm enjoying the gift more and more every day. God has honored my step of faith, and He is walking beside me, revealing his Plan as I trust and push.

I've painted the whole picture as I've experienced it for thirty-eight years. How many more layers I have yet to add and details to implement, only the Lord knows.

But I'll create until the end. In unique, broad strokes. Because it's part of my life portrait, the portrait of an artist with epilepsy.

Acknowledgments

I WANT TO thank God for giving me a full life, a story to tell, and talents to share. I also want to thank my family and friends, who offered insight and refreshed my memory on life events I had forgotten and that ultimately added dimension to my tale.

Made in the USA
Middletown, DE
24 February 2022

61650261R00125